¿QUÉ?

Costa Rica, Panama, Chile

Footloose Geezers Vol. II

By Allan D. Brown

ABCOM PUBLISHING

¿QUÉ? Costa Rica, Panama, Chile

Footloose Geezers Vol II

ISBN: 978-0-578-78925-5

ALSO BY ALLAN BROWN

NEWS-DAZE (2006) A novel

**BERKELEY-DAZE:
Memoir of a Frat Boy (2007)**

**SUN-STRUCK:
Growing up in Postwar California (2008)**

**CALIFORNIA SPLIT:
Racing through the Sixties (2009)**

**FOOTLOOSE GEEZERS:
Travels through Europe & Down Under
(2013)**

**AIX—'61: FRAT BOY GOES TO FRANCE:
An Approximate Memoir (2017)**

**BOSTON BAKED (2018):
Adventures in TV News & Other Exploits**

**Africa:
Around the Edges (2020)**

All are available on Lulu.com

Dedicated to those looking for Paradise.

CHAPTERS

PART I: COSTA RICA

PART II: PANAMA

PART III: CHILE

PROLOGUE

Sometime in early 2012, my wife Yvonne and I were sitting around in our home in Chicago wondering where to go next. We had been traveling quite a bit over the past few years, several times to Europe, including Greece and Turkey. Once to Australia and New Zealand. Also, we had made marathon drives around the U.S. supposedly seeking out a new retirement home—East Coast, West Coast, Rocky Mountains and the old South. All had their good points and all had their charms. At various times, we had seriously considered retirement in France, Australia or New Zealand. But we had yet to explore one of the most heralded retirement meccas of all, namely Costa Rica and Panama. We were lured by the siren song of cheap living in a tropical paradise. Americans were especially welcome. And the governments of both Costa Rica and Panama made it easy for retirees to live there in terms of immigration and a lack of red tape.

Of course, there was the question of why move at all. Chicago had much to offer, mainly the perks of city living. A safe and dynamic downtown (The Loop) with scads of cultural attractions like the Field Museum, the Art Institute, the Chicago Symphony and the Chicago Opera and of course, the Chicago Cubs in their yesteryear stadium. This along with great architecture and restaurants. And best of all, where we lived in an upscale section of Chicago called Edgebrook; was only twenty minutes from O-Hare airport in case we wanted to get out of town. All of the proceeding was true, but we were tired of it. After all, we had spent forty years here, the prime of our lives.

When we had arrived in 1971, I was in my early 30s, Yvonne in her late 20s. We had had pretty good careers here. Me, as a television news writer and producer at the ABC owned and operated station, WLS-TV. Yvonne as head art librarian at the Chicago Public Library. We both managed to retire with pensions and had decent 401K savings. I was in my early 60s, Yvonne in her late 50s. But after ten years here as retirees, we felt it was time to move on. After all, we were not really Chicagoans. I was from California originally. Yvonne was from Holland. We had met at UC Berkeley in 1967. After our marriage, we had set out on a footloose voyage that took us far from California—first to Europe, then New York, then Boston and finally Chicago. Essentially, we were living like gypsies until we got bogged down in Chicago. Oh well. It was here that we had our two offspring—Vanessa, now in medical residency in Colorado and Colin now living at home after graduating from Davidson College in North Carolina.

The other motivating factor to get out of town was the question of housing expenses. Our place needed at least a 100K upgrade in order to get top dollar and to take advantage of our desirable location on the far northwest side of Chicago. Edgebrook and Sauganash was where the Cook County and City judges lived along with high-level Chicago cops and firemen, this mainly because of the city residency requirement. It was a suburban atmosphere with upscale housing that was constantly being remodeled to even grander properties. As a result, property taxes were going up fast.

To keep up I would have to deal with a re-finance again. We had done that bit in 2003 for a new bathroom, a new roof, etc. And back in 1995, a new kitchen which needed to be remodeled again. Fuck it! I decided. When we sell, we will sell "as is." We had to get out of Dodge. Thus, our focus on Central America as the new "retirement paradise." So after a month of planning and setting everything up, we flew out of Chicago on Copa Airlines mid-April winging our way to Costa Rica and Panama. Here's how that went.

PART I: COSTA RICA

1. SAN JOSÉ

Tuesday, April 17

We caught an early morning flight from O'Hare on Copa Airlines with a stopover in Panama City and then on to San José, Costa Rica. We landed around 4 p.m. local time, whereupon I picked up a pre-paid rental a car through Europcar near the airport. This turned out to be a little VW hatchback with a scrape on the rear fender which I pointed out to the clerk. According the hustlers who ran this place, this was the only rental they had at my price level. It was take it or leave it. Unless of course, I wanted a much more expensive rental. But no free upgrade, don't you know. So despite the dent, I took it. Also, it was growing late and we wanted to check into our nearby hotel, Hotel Aeropuerto.

When we arrived there, we checked into a charming, laid-back hotel in the old Colonial style set in a maze of jungle landscaping with a kidney-shaped pool.

Hotel Aeropuerto

Wednesday, April 18

The next morning, we drove our shabby VW into San José and proceeded to get lost in a maze of streets before we stumbled onto the main plaza. Our initial impression driving around was that San José was a dump—crowded, shabby, and dirty with horrendous, honking traffic.

However, once we parked and started walking around, we discovered that the main plaza did have some scruffy charm. But it sure needed a power wash. Bird shit was on everything. The two main tourist attractions on the plaza—the Gold Museum and the old National Theater were closed. Apparently, the Gold Museum was a big deal featuring priceless pre-Columbia gold artifacts and early colonial gold pieces

After walking around the central plaza for a bit, we repaired to the Gran Hotel Costa Rica at one end of the plaza for a coffee.

Gran Hotel Costa Rica

This hotel still retained its old colonial atmosphere with lots of memorabilia about from the good old days of dominance by the United Fruit Company. We sat down at a café table with a view of the plaza and ordered coffee and a sweet roll. After that, we decided to have a small guaro sour, the national drink. This in honor of our arrival in Costa Rica. Mmmm…tasty indeed.

Following our morning snack, we hired an English speaking tour guide from the Gran Hotel to show us around the suburbs of San José. With Ricardo in the front seat and me driving our VW, he directed us to the suburb of Escazú. This suburb was home to the wealthiest and most prominent citizens in Costa Rica including wealthy Americans and Europeans. Driving through it, we did notice an abundance of upscale shops and restaurants. The homes we passed were nice as well, many two and three-story mansions. However, all the homes were heavily gated with high walls topped by razor wire. According to Ricardo, burglaries were rampant in Costa Rica. Earlier, we had noticed that all hotels and public buildings had armed security guards. Where were the peace-loving Costa Ricans?

We had been driving around for about an hour when we passed by a beautiful, brand new soccer stadium. When I pointed it out, Ricardo said it had been built by the Chinese. In turn, the Chinese had been allowed to set up massive distribution centers for their goods for the Central Americas. A tit for tat arrangement apparently.

Soccer Stadium

That night after dinner at the hotel, I left Yvonne in our room (she had pleaded fatigue) and went out to see what I could see. Coming in earlier I had noticed an interesting looking bar/roadhouse about a hundred yards down the road from the hotel. Sure enough, unlike the hotel lounge, this joint was jumping with a little band and what looked to be gigantic margaritas. Further, it was filled with an interesting assortment of people—the young, the beautiful (some dancing) and a surprising number of hip-looking seniors with younger women.

I scoped out the scene and then headed for the bar, a beautiful, carved mahogany bar, long and wide. I pulled up a barstool and ordered one of those large margaritas that I saw everywhere.

As I sipped away, I kept hearing the phrase "Pura Vida," almost like a chant from the bar patrons raising their glasses as if in a toast. What was that? I wondered. "Pure life?" I deduced from my limited Spanish. But I wasn't sure, so I asked an American looking guy sitting next to me. He looked at me and shrugged.

"Pura Vida? Yes, my friend," he said, "That means "hang loose, relax, no worries, no fuss, enjoy life. Be thankful for what you have and not dwell on the negative. ."

"Sounds like a recipe for good living," I replied.

"That it is. That it is," he nodded. "It's one of the main reasons I moved down here from the States."

"Really? I heard that most Americans move down here because it is cheap and they can live well on a modest income."

"That is certainly true but the lure of casual, easy tropical living is certainly a factor. Take me, I have been down here for three years and now rarely go back to the States. I have everything I need here including female companionship. All tucked away in a neat little house nearby that I bought for a song. By the way, my name is Paul," he said extending his hand for a shake.

As I shook his hand I introduced myself as well, "Glad to meet you, Paul. I'm Allan. My wife and I are here for a couple of weeks to see if we are interested enough to move down."

"Yes, yes. More and more Americans are moving here as well as many Europeans. I decided to live permanently here following my divorce in the states. That' fuckin' alimony was killing me even on a good government pension. I still pay it but it's much easier on my budget by living here. And as I said, no single American male will lack for female companionship here. The women are very accommodating if you treat them well.

I looked Paul over. He appeared to be a well-preserved sixty-something gentleman sporting a raffish goatee, still in good shape. Not fat at all. Sort of like me except I had no goatee.

We chatted on about life in Costa Rica for expats while I continued to sip on my never-ending margarita, eventually becoming quite bombed. And with the music and noise, the bar starting to spin in my head, I decided that I should head back to the hotel or maybe stagger back, whatever the case might be.

Thursday, April 19

The next morning we decided to explore the mountainous region around San José. Our goal was to take a look at a nearby local volcano, Barva Volcano, some 48 kilometers northeast of town. It seemed like an easy thing to do. But my Garmin GPS didn't work worth a shit as I drove along, constantly telling me "no map available." So I wandered through in one confusing little village after another chocked full of traffic.

Finally, we spotted a road sign that pointed the way to the Barva Volcano so we followed that. But as we climbed, the paved road soon ended and we were now on gravel and dirt with another sign recommending four-wheel drive only in the rainy season. This wasn't the rainy season but driving a rental car, I was still concerned with the road condition, rutted, bumpy, and with major potholes here and there. Plus, according to my guidebook, we would have to park three kilometers from the volcanos itself and hike in. That didn't seem worth the trouble.

However, up here at altitude, the air was clear and fresh with no hint of a tropical climate at all. It was invigorating so we descended a bit and drove around checking out the mountainous scenery and picturesque coffee farms along the way. Perfect hillside slopes for growing coffee. We returned to the hotel around one and hit that kidney shaped pool that I had thought we would never get a chance to use. An afternoon swim with another large margarita at our side was just what the doctor ordered. Tomorrow: Arenal, home to the largest active volcano in Costa Rica.

2. ARENAL VOLCANO

Friday, April 20

Up early, we drove north to San Ramón, a rather picturesque town tucked away in a valley and then took the turnoff to Arenal. Soon we were on a winding, narrow highway going through mountainous, jungle-covered terrain, interspersed with small villages and shacky houses situated almost right on the roadway. Hard to believe that this was the route to one of the major tourist attractions of Costa Rica. The saving grace was that this road was paved but it still took three hours to cover the 135 kilometers to Arenal.

We finally arrived at our destination around noon. We checked into our hotel, the Arenal Lodge, situated up on a hill with a commanding view of the countryside and most importantly, a great view of the Arenal Volcano, a picture-perfect cone about 2500 meters high (8,200 feet.)

The hotel itself was a throwback to a hill station right out of a Joseph Conrad novel—all teak wood, slow-moving fans, lots of jungled grounds and as we discovered later a pretty good dining room and bar and an infinity pool that was cool to swim in.

Arenal Lodge

Infinity Pool

Before relaxing at the hotel, we decided to explore around a bit and head over to the volcano. The hotel clerk had told us this was the time to do it because the peak of Arenal was clear today. Often it was shrouded in clouds or fog. So we took his advice and drove over to near the base of the volcano.

Arenal Volcano

We pulled into a parking lot and consulted a tourist map that had marked hiking trails around the base of the volcano. Indeed, a sign in the parking lot had the same trail map but also a warning that one should not try to hike to the top of the volcano. In fact, it was forbidden because Arenal was still an active volcano that was known to erupt now and then.

Indeed in 2000, it had a major eruption and a group of hikers near the peak of the volcano were killed by the spurting lava, ash, gas, and rocks tumbling down, some the size of trucks. Then there was a more recent eruption in 2010 but nobody was killed in that one. So here it was 2012, only two years later and no one knew when it would blow again. However, the clerk had also told us if the price was right, he could get a guide to lead us to the top and that the crater was a sight to see. We begged off, saying we were too old and too wise to risk being done in by a volcano.

What we did do was take a little hike around on one of the trails through the thick jungle that surrounded the base of Arenal. However, after hiking a kilometer or so, we realized that our view of the volcano was continually cut off by the jungle vegetation. So really this hiking was a waste of time.

We were about ready to turn around and head back to the car when we spotted a high, barbed wire fence with a gate marked "Danger—Off limits to Hikers" in both Spanish and English. The problem was just beyond the fence was a wide-open field which would surely give me a good view of the whole volcano, top to bottom. I managed to slip through a gap in the gate with my camera and hiked about a hundred yards or so along the trail, all the while snapping photos of the volcano, free and clear. Then at the urging of Yvonne who had stayed behind, I backtracked and cleared the fence just in time to see a tour group of hikers led by a local ranger on the same trail that led to the fence.

We nodded to them as they passed while we headed back to the parking lot. I suspected that the ranger had a key to the gate to give his hikers a privileged view of the volcano. A view that I had captured on my own with my trusty little Casio point-and-shoot camera by slipping through the gate.

Forbidden Way

Back at the hotel, we lounged around the pool and then had dinner in candlelight with a glow emanating from Arenal. Afterward, we slipped into the infinity pool and watched the glow still emanating from Arenal, now spiced up a bit by lightning in the far distance creating a primordial light show.

3. CLOUD FOREST

Saturday, April 21

The next morning we were picked up by the Desafio Adventure Company to take us to the Monteverde Cloud Forest. This involved taking a ferry across Lake Arenal and then traveling by minivan for over a rutted dirt road up to the cloud forest at Monteverde. Along the way, we traveled through what looked like the Dogpatch of Costa Rica. Of course, there were the ubiquitous mongrel dogs, chickens and occasional pigs wandering around. I noticed that while the city and suburban Costa Rican dwellers appeared middle class, the countryside folks were mostly poor-looking peasant types.

We arrived late afternoon at the town of Monteverde. It looked like a regular tourist trap with hotels and tour come-ons, etc. Where was the pristine cloud forest? Checking my guide, it turned out there were five of them, all privately owned but under the environmental control of the Costa Rican government.

Our tour activity for our day of arrival was a mountain bike jaunt. Yvonne with her sensitive back begged off. I was game and handed old mountain bike by our guide. It was truly hard on the ass as I went up and down a modest jungle trail over a very bumpy path. This reminded me of my days as a 12-year-old riding my bike on old fire trails in the hills around my home in Martinez, California. However, at age 72, I found this mountain biking less than a thrill and as noted, hard on the butt so after a couple of kilometers or so, I cut it short and walked my bike back. So much for mountain biking, a sport which still leaves me mystified. It's 12-year old stuff.

Later around 6 p.m. we went out on a jungle night hike led by a young botanist. This was a rather interesting hike with the guide pointing out all the nocturnal critters scurrying about, critters like the agouti—a cat-sized rat and a horned owl plus all kinds of insects buzzing about. Luckily, no mosquitoes. Supposedly Monteverde is too high up for them.

A further note here about the Agouti. As one description put it, an Agouti is a member of the rodent species, similar to a large guinea pig but with longer legs and a short, hairless tail. The Agouti varies in color from grey-tinged beige to a rich dark brown. They have coarse hair which rises when the animal is alarmed, making this rodent look even larger. The average length is around 20 inches, with a top weight of 18 pounds. And guess what? They are eatable, said to be very tasty when cooked right. Mostly consumed in Latin American countries.

Costa Rican Agouti

We stayed that night at the Hotel Montana, a big barn of a place that catered to large tour groups. This night the place was inundated by private school kids from Arizona on a spring break eco-tour. At first, they struck me as entitled little jerks on an expensive spring break. But after talking to a few of the young teenagers, we discovered that they were nice and very serious about environmental concerns. Later, we had a delicious chicken rice dinner washed down with beer.

Sunday, April 22

Up early for a morning tour of the Monteverde Cloud Forest. The guide, Antonio, led us on a mile walk through the jungle pointing out the various flora and fauna including bugs, strangler figs, monkeys, birds, and an occasional agouti. The cloud forest was indeed impressive but not as impressive as the Daintree ancient forest in Queensland, Australia that we had visited a few years earlier. There were no elevated catwalks, nor a tower from which to view the canopy. The reason for the cloud forest's existence, of course, was the moisture from the Pacific hanging about the mountain and hilltops in a more or less permanent cloud.

Cloud Forest Tour

At the end of the tour, we talked to Antonio about life in general in Costa Rica. He was an easy-going, portly fellow. I asked how come few Costa Ricans immigrated to the U.S. He explained that most Costa Ricans were happy here: "This is their little home, and most people have employment, a pension, free health care and no taxes to support a national army." He continued, "I am happy here. I don't want to leave. I like my job. I like my life." Thus spake Antonio, a happy man.

Later that morning, we went to nearby Selvaterra Park for a zip-line experience, an experience that Costa Rica is renowned for. Yvonne skipped the zip line thing and hiked around the park instead. Since it was included in our tour, I duly signed up, signed my releases and then trekked off with the zip-line group. We climbed up a steep hill, then a ladder up a massive tree to a wide platform. There we got instructions on how to zip-line without killing ourselves. Since I was the big guy, 6′2″, 240 pounds, I was given an extra belt for support. The whole rig involved a roller pulley device attached to the zip-line cable and a harness seatbelt contraption which in turn was attached to the roller pulley device via a carabiner. Added to this was a crash helmet.

The zip line procedure went like this. First, one guide would zip across to the next station while another stayed back on the departing platform to aid us zip-line neophytes. I stood back and watched a couple of young women people push off and zip along the line high over the jungle, screaming all the way until they safely arrived at the other platform. Swell, that was encouraging.

Next up was me. Securely strapped in, I pushed off. "Whee." I was on my way zipping along, trying to keep my feet straight and not swing from side to side. Along the way, I barely got a glimpse of the jungle beneath so concerned that I was about being steady. It was all such a rush I couldn't see anything much, all a blur.

Not Me

I made to my first destination station in good style. Others followed and on and on we went for several more different zip-line runs. The last zip line run was a kilometer long over a deep valley. This one took a long time for the zip line voyage and I did manage to take a good look down into the valley about a hundred feet below. It was then that the thrill and the utility of zip lining hit home. The only downside in this kilometer-long zip was I lost momentum about ten meters short of the station and the guide had to come out and rescue me.

In short, zip-lining was a thrill experience, sort of like hanging it all out on a roller coaster without the roller coaster. But you travel much too fast to see much. Originally, zip lining was a way for tree botanists to get from one canopy to another without climbing down. I noted that the guides were very good, lithe, strong quick fellows and at one in the trees. I also witnessed a German guy zip-lining with his three-year-old daughter strapped to his lap. A macho asshole indeed, but the kid seemed to like it. "Please daddy, do it again."

Later that afternoon, on our way back to Arenal we passed through a small Quaker settlement. They were all out milling around being sociable kids, mothers, dads and elders, all white Anglo Saxon looking, blond and blue eyed.

The guide told us they were all originally from the U.S. According to him, the Quakers immigrated here in the early 1950s to escape paying taxes to the U.S. war machine and to escape the draft for the Korean War. Once here they bought up land including land in the cloud forests and then cleared a lot of it for farming and raising dairy cows. Some of the land they kept in their original state for parks and tourist attractions. Still, it was weird to see the blond blue-eyed Quakers here in Costa Rica all speaking Spanish, some of whom I suspected could not even speak English.

4. ANTONIO PARK

Monday, April 23

After another great night at Arenal Lodge, we headed to Manuel Antonio National Park. This was a day-long drive down the same shitty highway as before leading to San Ramón. Since San Ramón was being touted as a retiree's paradise, we stopped and took a look around. The retirement development that we saw didn't consist of much other than vacant lots with views of the surrounding hills and mountains. Here and there was a newly constructed but modest-looking house but no one was in sight. Overall, it looked pretty barren to me

On to Punta Arenas. Now we were on the Pan American Highway and the going was much faster. Punta Arenas is a service town on the Pacific coast and the main port for Costa Rica. Overall, the town situated on a jut of land looked rather industrial. However, at the main dock, we did see a lot of very sleek, high powered fishing boats attesting to the fact that Punta Arenas was the jumping-off point for spectacular sport fishing.

Continuing down the coastal highway, we went through Jaco, a well-developed beach town. It looked O. K. but busy and hectic with flocks of tourists crowding the main streets in beach gear. A glance at the beaches reminded me of Coney Island with the mobs of people racked out in the sun.

Further down the coast past Quepos, we came to Manuel Antonio Park a jungled peninsula renowned for its rain forest, beaches and monkeys. We checked into Hotel Costa Verde set on the heights overlooking the Pacific but still in the midst of the forest. Being late afternoon, we didn’t do much except hit the hotel pool and lounge about, admiring the views. That night we ate at the hotel.

Tuesday, April 24

We spent the next morning hiking in the park. We had no guide so we wandered around on various trails getting hot and sweaty. Along the way, we saw a lot of squalling monkeys jumping around in the trees. Eventually, we came out onto a pristine beach scattered with bathers. It did look inviting and like a good snorkeling spot but we hadn't brought beach gear along so we hung around for a while, lounging under a shade tree viewing the scene and then trudging back to the parking lot.

Antonio Park

This side note: Earlier, before we found the actual entrance to the park, we got conned by a couple of roadside hustlers who waved us over into a pay parking lot. We stupidly paid them for parking and then were informed that we would be required to walk to the park a mile away or take a taxi for even more money. Sitting in our rental car for a few seconds, I figured out the con and demanded my money back and got it.

We then drove on another mile and there it was— a free parking lot right at the entrance of the park and not at all full. It was obvious the whole earlier scene was a rip-off.

After our little hike through Antonio Park, we returned to our room for a short while and then later in the afternoon, I went out to another nearby beach by myself and snorkeled around in the surf. I saw nothing but a sand bottom but that was O.K. I wasn't expecting much. Afterward, I lay out on the beach and got sunburned.

Meanwhile, back at the hotel room, Yvonne had been sitting out on the balcony when she was visited by a cute, little white-faced monkey. She said "Hello" and before she knew a whole troop of white-faced monkeys was swinging down from an adjacent tree just to put on a show for Yvonne and maybe beg for some food. The whole thing soon turned into a monkey jamboree with the monkeys prancing around on the balcony squealing, arguing, and fighting among themselves for attention. Finally, it got to be too much for Yvonne, almost scary so she went back in the room and closed the glass door on the critters that soon dispersed.

Wednesday, April 25

We decided to stay another day in Antonio Park since it was my "almost birthday," April 27th. In the morning we drove out of the park, checking out the wider scene. We noticed a lot of luxury condos going up. Overall it appeared that this region was slated for big-time development.

We then stopped at a big resort hotel at the tip of the peninsula, called Parador Resort & Spa. This was quite a layout with three pools, one reserved for adults, endless jungle landscaping punctuated by various fountains and a great view of the Pacific crashing below on the rocks. Reportedly, there was a pet boa constrictor that wandered about the resort but we didn't see it. Nice digs if you could afford it

Back at our hotel, we spent the rest of the day at the hotel pool under an umbrella. Forget the beach. It looked nice from a distance but I had to lounge in the shade after my sunburn yesterday.

That evening we dressed up in our tropical best—me in white slacks, shoes and a Tommy Bahama tropical shirt. And Yvonne in an elegant tropical white dress with an orchid behind her right ear to signal she was available. (Just joking) After teasing me, she changed the flower to her left ear, signaling that she was taken.

El Avion Restaurant

We then proceeded to dine at the nearby El Avion Restaurant which featured an old C-123 cargo plane jutting out from its exterior, like something out of a Jimmy Buffet fantasy.

Word was that this plane was used in the U.S. sponsored Contra operations against the Sandinista government in neighboring Nicaragua in the 1980s. The cool thing was that it housed a bar right inside the superstructure of the plane, thus fully integrating it into the restaurant.

For dinner, we both started off with a strong and tasty Piña Colada. We then had as our main dish a perfectly grilled red snapper with sides of fried plantains and other vegetables—all downed with steins of the local beer. All in all, a perfect birthday dinner for me even if it was two days early.

5. THE CONDO

April 26—May 3

The next morning we drove back to San José for our rendezvous with the high rise condo that we had rented for a week near the town of San Rafael. The town was a dump but we found our two-bedroom condo in a park-like area outside of town. It turned out to be very sleek and modern with a view of the mountains and a heart-shaped pool below with a sheltered barbeque area.

Condos

Our condo interior featured air-conditioning, a well-appointed kitchen, a combination living room/dining room with lime green walls, a black leather sofa and easy chairs. In the center was a glass-top dining room table. The two bedrooms were small but had comfortable looking queen size beds. The bathroom and shower were lined with lime green designer tile as well, still very clean and sleek.

"Yes," we thought. "Despite all the lime green, this would do nicely. Live like a middle-class Costa Ricans for a week to see if we really wanted to settle here."

Our Condo

We immediately set up shop and drove to the nearest Walmart for supplies. Rather than hitting a bunch of local shops for this and that, Walmart had it all in one location. Normally, I am not a big Walmart fan but the one we encountered in the nearby suburb of Escazú was rather upscale and had everything that we needed. Their stuff was also expensive by Costa Rican standards. In any case, thank god for Walmart.

Once settled in our condo, we hit the pool and lounged about having it all to ourselves. But then this was a Thursday. However, come Friday afternoon and all through the weekend, the pool area was jammed with kids and families apparently visiting friends and relatives who lived in the condo complex.

The kids and the parents would arrive around ten a.m. and stay all day until the early evening, barbequing, drinking and playing loud music until ten or so. This was annoying and we stayed away but we also got a close-up view of middle-class Costa Ricans. They were nice but noisy and very family-oriented and very into the material thing judging by all water accouterments.

The other hitch occurred when the lady landlord dropped by to see how we were doing and noted that both bedrooms had been used. In her broken English, she claimed that she had rented us only one bedroom. I told her as far as I was concerned I had paid for the entire condo, not just one bedroom. I showed her my rental agreement. It said nothing about using only one bedroom. In any case, I explained that I snored sometimes and often slept in a separate bedroom in order not to disturb my wife. That more or less shut her up and she retreated down the hall mumbling in Spanish.

During that week, we did become better acquainted with the surrounding area. One day while driving around, we took a closer look at San Rafael. It wasn't much but it did give you an idea of a typical small-time Costa Rican town.

San Rafael

We also noted that our condo complex was near a major San José prison, a forbidding looking place with high electrified fences and guard towers everywhere. Also, when we drove in and out of our condo complex, we noticed that the security guard at the entrance gate was equipped with what looked like an AK-47. That was unnerving and made us wonder about the crime and security around this place.

Still, Costa Rica wasn't as bad as their next-door neighbor,

Nicaragua. One day while walking outside the condo grounds, it started to rain so I sat down in bus stop kiosk to wait it out. Seconds later, a cute cleaning girl sat down next to me waiting for her bus. To pass the time we started talking in my limited Spanish. She said she was from neighboring Nicaragua and had come to Costa Rica to work and also to escape the rampant crime there. She said Costa Rica was a "Paraisio" compared to Nicaragua and that many "Nicas" came here to escape that and to work.

***

However, none of the darker side of Costa Rica slowed us down during our week in the condo. We made several extended excursions into the nearby countryside. The first was a trip to another local volcano, the Irazu Volcano. Unlike our earlier efforts at volcano viewing, this was one a success because I could drive up to it on paved roads. Still, it took two hours to make it to the top. Once there we peered down into one of the three craters that comprised the volcano, one with a lake in it. We then hiked around nearby ash and lava fields. The locals claimed the Irazu Volcano was still active, but it looked pretty dead to us. But hey, we had made it to the top of a Costa Rican volcano without hiking our asses off.

Irazu Volcano

Another day we drove through Santa Ana another upscale suburb similar to Escazú. Although Santa Ana was much smaller and more picturesque than Escazú, it was said to be quite popular with expats since it featured many great restaurants, shops and a very expensive shopping mall called the Multiplaza Shopping Mall.

As we approached the mall, we could see it was indeed mammoth. Something like the mega-malls in the Los Angeles area. We parked and got out to explore the mall and it was indeed impressive with its shops of leather goods and jewelry. Also, many American brand name shops like North Face, Levis and Tommy Hilfiger. In addition, the mall was spacious with a grand vaulted ceiling from which hung a variety of ornamentation.

Multi Plaza Mall

Best of all, the mall provided air-conditioned relief from the muggy heat outside. It was hard to drag Yvonne out of there even though she bought nothing.

"Just looking," she insisted and then added, "I can get this stuff much cheaper in Chicago."

I waited her out by sitting down at an ice cream café and having large ice cream soda.

***

On another day we once again ventured a drive into downtown San José. I was initially reluctant but Yvonne was hell-bent on seeing the Museum of Contemporary Art and Design. Caving in, I did manage to navigate the downtown traffic in good order but when I arrived at the museum parking lot, it was all jammed up. However I did find one tight, open spot next to a wall. I pulled in and then jockeying for a better angle, I backed up. It was then I heard a grind on my rear fender. Shit! I had scraped the wall. I got out and inspected.

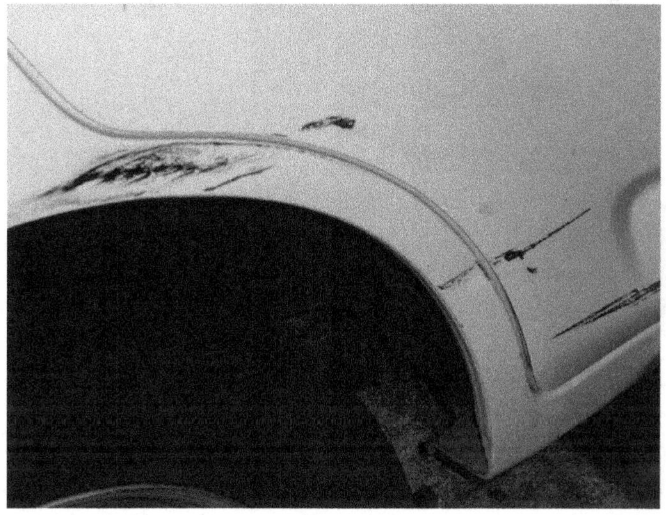

Rear Fender Scrape

Guess what it didn't look too bad. The new scrape was right over the old scrape that the car had when I rented it. Since I had not taken extra coverage due to my American Express coverage, I thought no big deal. First, those car rental guys would probably not notice a new scape over the old scrape and second I was covered anyway. All was good or so I thought. In any case, after cussing me out about the new scrape, Yvonne hustled off to the museum with me following her like a beaten dog.

Guess what, the museum was rather charming and well worth a look. It featured some nine hundred works of art by the outstanding artists of Spain, Costa Rica and other Central American countries. This included paintings, sculpture, photography, various installation and video art. All very impressive. The paintings were a mix of styles ranging from cubistic to primitive, most depicting scenes and life from the streets and nature of Central America.

Art & Design Museum

While we were staying at the condo we did explore a nearby retirement community. It had the standard golf course, pool and big houses going for a 400-thousand and up. Here you could live like an American. But ultimately, the question for us was would we want to retire in Costa Rica or even spend a few months here?

First, at our immediate surroundings, the weather was pleasant, not too hot at about 1000 meters in elevation, much cooler than along the coast but still never changing. There are no real seasons in Costa Rica, only a rainy season and a not so rainy season.

Second, the cost of living like a gringo in Costa Rica was about the same as the U.S. in many states such as Nevada, Idaho and Utah. An average model U.S. style home here went for about 250-300K. You do get a break in that you can hire cheap help and dine on cheap food if you buy on the local economy. Also, adequate medical care is cheap but note that Medicare does not work here. You have to pay out of pocket. For major operations, most American expats fly back to the states in order to be covered by Medicare.

Add to that, other than the bar crowd that I met, most of the retired American expatriates that we met were boring. Based on what we saw visiting these few retirement communities, most just sit in their houses and vegetated in the air-conditioning. Oh, an active few did appear to get out to golf and go fishing or go shopping or simply lounge around the pool with fellow American expatriates, drinking. Few spoke Spanish since all the Costa Ricans that they came in contact with already spoke fluent English.

But wait, you say. What about all the natural splendors of Costa Rica —the volcanos, the cloud forests, the scenic pristine beaches of the Pacific, the surfing paradise spots. Aren't they enough to keep you enchanted? Maybe. And it is also true that we had only seen a modest portion of what Costa Rica had to offer.

However, all of that was tourist stuff or stuff for the young and adventurous. Usually, after a couple of months of running around enjoying the attractions, older expats simply retired to their homesteads and, as I said, vegetate.

So as we finally flew out following our two-week stay, we were hoping for a more enlightening time in Panama.

***

But wait! I have to describe what happened to us turning the rental car in with the scraped rear fender. At first, one of the Europcar dudes gave it a glance and then a nod and it appeared that we were good to go but then the supervisor came out and took a look, focusing on the scrape.

He then turned to me and said in very good English, "Señor Brown, we did note the original scrape on the rear fender when you took it out two weeks ago but now I see worse damage in the same spot with a longer scrape. Here, I can show the difference because we photographed the original scrape after it occurred. He showed me a photo on his cell phone. What do you say about that?

I replied, "It all looks the same to me. A scrape over a scrape on the same spot would still require the same repairs, probably at the same cost."

"Yes," he countered, "but I am sorry. We will have to charge you for further damage. It will go on your credit card, for probably around $ 500 U.S."

"Hold on," I protested. "I have American Express car rental collision coverage. They will take care of it. You don't have to charge me anything."

"Well, I will have to verify that before we can proceed," he huffed. "A lot of people claim that."

"Go ahead, but be quick," I urged. "We have a plane to catch."

He nodded, returned to the office and phoned American Express on their international number. And we waited and waited for him to get through. Finally, after ten minutes or so he got someone on the line that did indeed verify that I had this coverage. I talked to the American Express rep. too and he assured me of the coverage. I thought that would be the end of the story. But nooo. The supervisor said he still had to charge me even though American Express would reimburse me at some point.

"Bullshit!" I exclaimed. "They said they would pay it off. There's no reason to charge me."

At that point, he pulled out the full contract of the rental agreement and pointed to a fine print section that granted Europcar the right to charge for full damages even if there is third party coverage. Then he intoned, "You are lucky Senor Brown that I did not charge you with the full charge that we are allowed, many thousands of dollars. Of course, you would eventually get it all back."

"Yeah in the meantime, I have a shitload load of credit card debt until American Express kicks in," I sneered.

He nodded and walked off. I knew I was beaten. I guess I was lucky that he was only going to charge me for 500 bucks. Anyway, I didn't have time to dicker. Our flight time was drawing near. As we headed towards the airport in a taxi, I vowed never to rent from Europcar again. A chickenshit operation indeed.

This postscript: American Express did cover me eventually. Then forgetting my experience with Europcar, I did rent from them again three years later in Chile and ran into yet another hassle. When will I learn?

PART II: PANAMA

1. PANAMA CITY

Thursday, May 3

Ola! We are now in Panama City which after the dump known as San José, looks like Dubai. Skyscrapers everywhere, very modern, with streets that are paved and well-marked. We are staying right downtown at the Four Points Sheraton.

Panama City

Tomorrow we will do the city tour. And on Saturday, we will take the Panama Canal transit tour, all the way from the Pacific Ocean to the Atlantic Ocean. My Spanish is picking up.

Friday, May 4

The city tour was a sort of a bust. The guide wasn't all that knowledgeable, although we did hit the highlights—the old city, Casco Viejo, the even older city of Panama Vieja, a couple of churches and the Panama Canal locks at Miraflores.

First, we headed to Casco Viejo in the historic district. Situated on a jut of land and separated from modern Panama City. Casco Viejo was declared a World Heritage Site by UNESCO back in the 1990s. In order to get into it, though, our driver had to pass by another district known as El Chorrillo which had been bombed to smithereens in 1989 during the U.S. invasion of Panama. From what we could see except for a few high rise apartment houses, this district of poverty has still not recovered.

El Chorrillo District

As we entered Casco Viejo, we had to navigate a series of narrow streets clogged with traffic until we came out on the main square dominated by the church, Iglesia La Merced.

Iglesia La Merced

Overall the ambiance of the 17th century Spanish architecture was charming with many restored buildings but also much of Casco Viejo was also a slum with ratty apartment buildings and crumbling exteriors, all decorated by hanging laundry.

Casco Viejo

As we drove around the restored section of the square, we noted several charming small hotels and interesting looking restaurants, one of which would eat at on another day. The capper to our tour of the old city was the waterfront that had been entirely renovated with wide concrete walkways and a low seawall. Here we got out of the car and once again took in spectacular views on the new modern Panama City with its forest of high rise apartment buildings and skyscrapers.

View from Casco Viejo

Following our brief tour of the old city, we headed over to the Miraflores Locks, the entrance to the Panama Canal. We parked and took a long flight of stairs up to the Miraflores Visitor Center observation deck from which we could view the locks. However, the observation deck was so crowded with tourists that at first we could barely see the ships entering the locks. But by pushing and jamming our way to the deck railing, we did manage to see the whole locking process. The two ships we did see negotiating the locks were guided by two steam engines that ran alongside on rails of the canal locks. Needless to say, it was a long, slow process.

Miraflores Locks

Later, we checked out the visitor center museum explaining the history of the canal. And while informative, I still thought the best way to understand the history of the canal was to read David McCullough's *Path Between The Seas*, which I had done a few years ago.

In any case, our time at the Miraflores Locks was only a brief preview of what we were in for the next day when we were going on a day-long boating excursion that would cover the entire length of the canal

Following Miraflores, we drove south of the city to view the 16th century ruins of a settlement even older than Casco Viejo, called Panama La Vieja. These were the ruins of the first Spanish settlement in Panama in the early 1500s and indeed the oldest European settlement on the Pacific coast of the Americas. As we wandered around the still intact ruins, you could see the settlement was laid out on a grid over several acres, perhaps an early example of town planning. Of course, the town was dominated by a church whose original walls were still standing.

Panamá la Vieja

Panamá la Vieja is also a UNESCO heritage site and as we wandered around, it felt like the original inhabitants were still somewhere about. A ghostly feeling, indeed.

Our tour guide soon drove us back downtown and let us off at our hotel. I didn't feel like tipping him much because he hardly spoke to us during the tour but I did anyway for public relations reasons.

Still not satisfied that we had seen all that we could see of Panama City, we set off wandering around the immediate area. A lot of building construction was going on. Cranes were everywhere hoisting steel girders up on high for high rise apartments and even more banks. And the main thoroughfares of the modern city, such as Via Israel were very busy with bumper to bumper traffic. Overall the newer Panama City struck us as a "bank city" with cocaine towers, sort of like a little Miami.

But when we cut through to the back streets, we got a glimpse of an older more gentile Panama City, very peaceful and noise-free. We admired the turn of the century Spanish architecture of the smaller business establishments and apartment houses all with lush landscaping, courtyards and gurgling fountains. This was the Panama City that we should have stayed in. Alas. However, the Four Points Sheridan was good enough, if somewhat past its prime. It was convenient and it did have a rooftop swimming pool with views of the city.

2. CANAL TRANSIT

Saturday, May 5

The canal transit tour. This was a big day. Up early,

5 a.m. and a taxi to the docks where the Carterra transit ship awaited. We were lucky to get on this tour because the full transit tour of the canal only happens a couple of times a month. We were going to see it all on a ten-hour journey one way, inch by inch.

Carterra

The Carterra was already jammed with people even at this early hour. We were able to get a table with a view of the canal but we had to share it Steve, a weird guy from Colorado. Steve said he worked in the fracking fields but had some time off. He sported long hair tied in a ponytail and a goatee, reminding me of a latter-day hippy. He told us he was traveling through Central America by bus on a two-week jaunt.

Despite his hippy demeanor, Steve was a die-hard Republican who hated Obama. "Fucker wants to shut down fracking on the Western Slope. It's a fuckin' bonanza out there. Cheap energy." Steve further added that he thought most of Central America a shithole. Other than that he was a fun guy.

After about an hour, our cruise got underway or almost underway. We had to wait for a large cargo ship to go through the first set of locks. It moved ahead slowly, very slowly, inch by inch with hardly any clearance on each side of the lock. Once it got through, it was our turn. Again, we moved ahead inch by inch into the first set of locks. Once inside the gates, the gates closed and the locks filled up with water, raising the ship eighty-five feet or so above sea level.

The whole process was so slow that I had plenty of time to examine these amazing locks. These were the original locks almost 100-years old, all very moldy and very mossy. All the while an annoying tour guide speaking over a loudspeaker filled us in on the history of the canal, something I already knew. Shut up, will you!

Miraflores Lock Gates

Once through the Miraflores locks, we set sail on a placid body of water for several kilometers called the Miraflores Lake. It was all peaceful and lulling until we reached a narrow section known as the Culebra Cut. This is where the engineers had to do a massive excavation to complete a narrow passage. The Culebra Cut didn't look like much top side; just a hill that went up in steps but most of the cut was underwater out of sight.

Culebra Cut

Along the way we observed construction crews, cranes and steam shovels widening and deepening the canal at various points. In addition, they were adding new locks adjacent to the old Miraflores locks. All of this was so that the larger ships could make the passage through the canal. Word was that the Chinese were financing most of it. Something that the Panamanians deny. They claimed that it was entirely Panama's show with financing from banks around the world.

At one point we passed by a Norwegian cruise ship slowly plodding along. We could see and hear the passengers who were hanging on the rails, drinks in hand, oohing and ahhing about the fact that they were crossing the Panama Canal, for many a lifetime dream.

Cruise Ship

But really, how much could they see from the high decks of the cruise ship. Certainly, not the intricacy of the locking system. I thought that being on a small transit boat allowed a much more intimate look and feel for the canal. Then there was the cost issue. Cruise ship passengers pay thousands of dollars for a cruise through the Panama Canal. We did it for less than a tenth of the cost and probably saw a lot more. Of course on a cruise ship, they probably stopped off at several Caribbean islands along the way and then at various ports of call going north along the Pacific coast.

Eventually, we came out to Lake Gatun, a large natural lake in the center of the Panama Isthmus with jungled islands, some a nature preserve. This was even more sleep-inducing but we fought off the drowsiness and just ate and drank along with the others. Finally, late afternoon we came to the Colon locks on the Atlantic side. These were more spectacular than the Miraflores locks. Because of our elevation, we could see and hear the water rushing out of the locks with an unobstructed view. The locks had to lower us some 80-feet to the Atlantic Ocean. Somehow this went faster. Finally out of the locks, we docked at the Colon waterfront. It looked spruced up for the tourists but the town itself was old, run-down and crime-ridden so they say.

Colon Waterfront

Once docked, we then boarded buses for the run back across the Isthmus to Panama City. Soon we were on an expressway barreling along making the 64-kilometer run from the Atlantic to the Pacific in just under an hour. Then it hit me. This is the only place in the western hemisphere where you can do that. Go from the Atlantic Ocean to the Pacific Ocean in an hour. As we buzzed along, I thought of the Spanish Explorers who dropped like flies while making this traverse which then took weeks of hacking through a fever-ridden jungle. Even with a railway built during the mid-19th century, the traverse took days. Panama was then a crossover point for those traveling to the goldfields of California.

All in all, it was a highlight day. We had traversed the Panama Canal. Stunning. Yes, it was an all-day venture; slow as molasses but still quite impressive going along the canal with the jungle closing in on either side, traversing Lake Gatun and on to Colon. However, I did notice that there was absolutely no security for this journey. There was no check of backpacks on the boat or any luggage for that matter. Who was watching? No one apparently.

3. BOQUETE

Sunday, May 6

The next morning we had a rental car delivered to the hotel and what a car it was! A brand new 2012 Nissan Pathfinder, a spacious four-wheel-drive vehicle. Now, this was the way to rent a car. No hassles at a rental desk, just a quick signature and we were good to go. Of course, it was expensive for ten days but after my experience with cheap-ass Europcar in Costa Rica, I went for Hertz. As it turned out, the Pathfinder was worth every penny.

Our mission today was to drive 500 kilometers northwest to a town called Boquete, reportedly a mini-paradise in the midst of hilly terrain full of coffee plantations. Getting there was an all-day journey, mostly on the legendary Pan American Highway sometimes through drenching downpours, all the time watching the speed limit and spotting cops on motorcycles huddled underneath the overpasses to stay out of the rain.

We hit the turnoff to Boquete at David, a rather large service town for the region. While passing through the outskirts, I wondered why a town in Hispanic Central America was called "David." At this point, I had no real answer for that. Maybe it was founded by a Gringo named David.

When we finally arrived in Boquete, we were met at the town square by one Howard Hilt, a longtime resident retiree, photographer and greeter. A slim, fit, sixties guy with a trim beard, Hilt was the caretaker of the house where we were going to stay.

Since it was already late afternoon, Howard suggested we buy some grocery supplies before heading up to the house. He would come along to show us the ropes but first, he gave us a short tour of downtown Boquete. It wasn't much but it did have a nice shady square where the locals hung out and indeed quite a few senior Anglos. Nearby was a small supermarket where under Howard's direction we stocked up on groceries including beer and margarita materials. After that, we followed Hilt in his VW up a series of hills to the house that was to be our home for a week.

After a lot of twists and turns on a narrow road, we arrived at our abode perched high up on a hillside with a steep drive. But, once negotiated and once out of the car, we were treated to some spectacular views of the mountainous hills and the lush valleys of the Boquete.

Our House

We went in with Howard and checked out our place for the next six nights. It was modern and spacious in a vaguely Hispanic way, appropriately furnished with overhead revolving fans. When Howard pointed out the fans, he declared that up at this altitude of 35-hundred feet there was no need for air conditioning. "Spring-like temperatures prevail throughout the year," he claimed.

We then went out back and took a look at the garden, very lush indeed and inviting with a winding concrete path leading to a couple of fountains and a little stream full of mossy rocks.

Back Garden

Following that, we enjoyed a beer with Howard sitting on the front balcony admiring the magnificent views of the mountains and valleys of Boquete.

View from our House

Later downstairs, as Howard was getting ready to leave, I noticed at the back of the carport what looked like a downstairs apartment.

"Yes, there is a downstairs apartment," said Hilt. "It currently has an occupant for an extended stay but Max shouldn't bother you much. He knows to leave the upstairs alone. He is some kind of techie that works from his apartment all day."

I thought this was a sour note. We might have to deal with a neighbor. Yvonne and I wanted only splendid isolation in this pristine environment. When I rented this place, no mention was made of what was essentially a basement apartment. Or maybe I missed it on the rental agreement due to my eagerness of getting a cheap price.

In any case, I just nodded at Howard's explanation and thanked him for babysitting us and getting us settled. As he was about to depart, he said he would be glad to meet up with us at the square tomorrow, show us some more of Boquete and then have lunch at a great little restaurant he knew that was very reasonable. We agreed to that and bid him goodbye, thinking that he was probably a very lonely guy here in this retirement paradise.

Back up at the house, Yvonne and I had a couple of strong pre-mixed margaritas on the front balcony watching the last remnants of the sunset. Afterward, we dined on stuffed tacos that Yvonne had prepared. Day one in Boquete over and out.

Monday, May 7

The next day, after a fried plantain and scrambled eggs breakfast, we were out and about fairly early. By the way, the eggs here were delicious, full of flavor and substance. Nothing like the weak watery versions that you get in the States. Anyway, we were off in our Pathfinder, making our way down the winding road to explore Boquete some more. Our mission was more than simple sightseeing. We were trying to determine if this was a viable retirement spot or not.

We took a slow drive through downtown. It struck us as rather ordinary with its two-story balconied buildings, sometimes painted in bright colors. Plenty of cars lined the main street and parking was tight.

Main Street, Boquete

Nonetheless, I found a spot, parked and went into a pharmacy to check out its offerings of prescription drugs, reputed to be a fraction of the cost of the same drugs in the U.S. That appeared to be true looking at the posted price list.

However, a young pharmacist lady who spoke perfect English told me that the one particular prescription pill that I took daily was not available. It had to be ordered from the U.S. at significant cost. Obviously, that would be a hassle. So much for prescription bargains for this retiree.

Moving on towards the outskirts of town, Yvonne spotted what appeared to be a brand new library. Of course, her being a former head art librarian in Chicago, we had to stop and check that out.

Boquete Library

We went in, nodded to a young American looking guy behind the reference desk and checked out the offerings. The collection was mostly popular biographies and best sellers both in English and Spanish. The library also had a nice collection of local art scattered throughout. As we turned to go, the librarian asked where we were from.

"Chicago. Just on a holiday here, checking out Panama."

"No kidding, I'm from Chicago too. I'm Luke."

"Really Luke, what are you doing here running a library? Don't they have Panamanian librarians here?" I inquired.

"Sure, but I'm here to give them a little help. This is what I did in Chicago. I worked at the UIC library for a while but got bored with that so I joined the Peace Corps and here I am"

"Nice gig for the Peace Corps," I replied. "At least you are not out in some jungle trying to put in water systems."

"Yeah, we do what we can. I do go out in the boonies with a bookmobile from time to time, but mostly I am here."

"We noticed a lot of books in English, is that because of the retiree community here?"

"Oh yeah, they are heavy users. Not much else to do around here except read. To me, it's kind of a boring life but the retirees appear to like it. Anyway, I have only a few more months around here and then I'm done with my tour."

"What are you going to do then?" I asked.

"I don't know. Travel around a bit in Central and South America. Eventually, I'll go back to Chicago for a while, get a job, check out my old girlfriends. Or maybe, I will re-up for the Peace Corps and go to some other interesting place."

"Well, good luck, Luke."

We bid him goodbye and moved on.

Next, we wanted to drive around and take a look at the real estate scene. However, no way did we want to a realtor involved. This would just be a curbside viewing excursion.

We drove further out of town and came to a retirement development known as Valle Escondido. We drove in through the manned security gate as if we belonged here with the guard waving us through.

Valle Escondido

Tucked away in a little valley, this place struck us kind of a Shangri-La. It reminded me of a Del Webb active adult community with luxury townhouses galore, some detached homes even more luxurious. Of course, a perfectly groomed golf course. We spotted a large community center that housed a fitness center and served several outdoor swimming pools. The denizens of this luxury retreat mostly moved about in golf carts staring at us with a stupefied but pleasant gaze as if they had just dined on Soma from Thomas Huxley's Brave New World. Contented as cows.

We headed back towards the entrance and parked in the visitor's center lot. But for some reason, it was still closed even though it was now 10 a.m. However, posted in the windows were scads of real estate offerings touting new townhouses in the upper 200-thousand dollars range and detached houses going for 400-thousand and more. Definitely not bargain-basement living in Panama. It was similar to what you would pay in the U.S.

We walked around a bit more, enjoying the parklike ambiance of the place. Temperatures were indeed spring-like in the 70s, with low humidity. The bees were buzzing and the birds chirping and here and there fountains were gurgling. All very enticing but not for us. We moved on.

About a mile down the road was roadside sign pointing to a new housing development up on a hill. In the low $100-thousands US, it said. O.K. we will check that out.

So I turned up the hill and followed the signs to a modest little development strung along the hillside. The houses looked small. We parked in the drive of what appeared to be a model home.

Typical New House

A gringo realtor was inside showing a prospective buyer the various attributes of the house.

"This place is a steal for only 100 grand," he proclaimed.

The potential buyer, a stocky blue-collar looking American replied, "Yeah but I heard that the best deal is to rent a place like this. I mean, I spend most of my time in the U.S. I hear you rent a house like this furnished for about a thousand a month."

"Maybe, but then there is nothing like owning."

Then turning towards us, the realtor asked, "How about you two? Come live in paradise."

"Don't look at us. We are just looking around trying to get a feel for the housing market here."

"Well, for what you would pay in the U.S.," the realtor replied checking out our new Pathfinder in the driveway,

"You could live like a king here."

I had to admit for a two-bedroom, one-bath house; this one was well put together with a spacious living/dining room area. An ultra-modern kitchen with the latest appliances and an attached garage. Best of all it had a wide veranda porch out back with a view of the valley and based on the lot size plenty of room for a swimming pool. It was tempting.

Still, seeing he wasn't getting anywhere with us, he excused himself to accost another couple who had just driven up. That left us along with the stocky guy.

So I asked, "You going to buy a place like this?"

"Naw, like you, looking around," he replied. "I've heard the best deal in Boquete is to rent. I have to spend most of my time in Austin, Texas running my plumbing business.

The only reason I'm down here is because my wife is from Panama and she gets homesick so I promised we would have a second home here. But I'm sold on renting not buying. I might sign a three-year lease on one of these houses. I hear you can furnish it on the cheap by going down to David's furniture warehouse.

"Sounds like a plan."

"Yeah, got to keep the little lady happy…."

Yvonne winced at that remark.

"And in any case, it is no big deal, I love Panama too," he continued. "We might retire here full time down the road. Of course, being away a lot, you got to have a security system and watch out for burglaries around here."

"Burglaries?"

"Yeah, there seems to be a rash of them these days. Many retirees have established a neighborhood watch of sorts but the police don't seem to do much about it. If someone is ripped off and even if they think they know who did it, the police do not pursue. 'What the fuck,' they apparently think. The rich gringos can afford it. No Boquete is a far from perfect place but it does come close."

"So you say," I replied, thinking that indeed no place is perfect.

***

After our brief glimpse into the real estate scene in Boquete, it was time for our lunch date with Howard Hilt. We drove back into town and sure enough there he was sitting in his little VW at the town square. I stopped, got out and approached him. He greeted me, shaking my hand through the turned down window as if we were old friends that had not seen each other for a while.

"Come on, it's time to eat. This is a great little place. Follow me," he urged.

I returned to the Pathfinder and did indeed follow him through the back streets of Boquete until we came to a little non-descript restaurant on a hidden side street. If you didn't know it was there you could easily miss it. We both parked and went inside. It was small with only four or five tables but pleasant with Boquete tourist posters plastering the wall and a slow revolving fan overhead to keep the place cool.

The proprietor, a pleasant, plump Panamanian lady, greeted Howard in rapid Spanish. Howard, in turn, responded in fluent Spanish. I could see that if you lived here you really had to learn Spanish in order to appreciate Panama, even though most spoke some English.

Once seated and served a round Balboa Beer, we looked over the offerings scrawled on a blackboard on the wall. It was all "pollo" this or "pollo" that. Howard said you could have anything you wanted here as long as it was chicken— barbequed, baked or fricasseed.

"It's all great," he insisted.

So we ordered barbequed chicken along with rice, plantains and other assorted vegetables. It took a while to arrive at our table but Howard was right, it was chicken like I had never tasted it before— sweet, full-flavored and juicy with a light barbequed crust.

I wondered aloud how come chicken in Central America was so good with the comment "Makes the U.S. variety taste like shit," I observed.

"Simple," replied Howard, "They are raised outdoors, cage-free as you would say. No antibiotics, all-natural food and no insistence on constantly laying eggs like in the states."

"Make sense. Score another plus for Panama."

"It's just one of the many benefits of living here," continued Howard.

"Oh yeah, cheap living and all. Is that why you are here?"

"Basically, like a lot of other retirees, I escaped to Panama after an expensive divorce and had to live on a reduced income. This place was a godsend for that. Fifteen hundred to two thousand bucks a month and you can live like a king here."

"Really? We saw some pretty expensive housing here at the Valle Escondido," I countered.

At this point, Howard opened up. "Yes, there is that. Living like a full-scale American here can be expensive. But for those on a budget, you can still live well. Rents are absurdly low for a nice tidy little house and healthy food in the local markets is dirt cheap. You also have free medical care by U.S. trained doctors, many of whom practice in nearby David. And if you budget right, you can indulge in a bit of modest travel. It's all very doable. I've been everywhere in Central America and a good portion of South America. I do a lot of travel photography for both Panama and other Central American countries."

Howard paused, and then with a slight smile continued, "Maybe the best part of living here for single men are the friendly Panamanian women. I have a great live-in girlfriend. Not a kid but in her 30s. Maybe we might even get married."

"Sounds like you have started a great second life," I observed.

"You got it. I feel reborn and definitely years younger."

On that note, I stopped being nosy about Howard's life here and we settled back and enjoyed another round of beer.

Eventually, Howard had to excuse himself saying he had some chores to run before he returned to his girlfriend in their little house. But before he left, he let us know about a weekly flea market that was to take place tomorrow at the community center.

"You don't want to miss this," he said. "The whole retirement community will be there, many of them hawking their wares. A lot do handicrafts, to say nothing of indigenous folks who do the same. Also, it's a great place to gather information about living in Boquete. Unfortunately, I have to go out of town for a few days, so I won't make it.

Howard also gave us a recommendation for a coffee tour outfit and with that he said goodbye and off he went. I caught the bill that was absurdly cheap and minutes later we were off too, first to arrange our coffee tour at a local tourist agency and then to negotiate that winding drive up the hill after a couple of beers. Still, we arrived safe and sound at our house on the hill.

As I parked in the drive, I noticed that the door of the downstairs apartment was open and a bearded guy in thongs and shorts was padding about. This was our downstairs neighbor. He nodded a greeting to us. I nodded back but then ignored him. Right then all we wanted was our upstairs refuge with the stunning views and nobody to bother us. Introductions can wait. Essentially, this was the end of day two in Boquete.

Tuesday, May 8

Following Howard's advice the next morning, we visited the weekly flea market at the community center. When we arrived there the place was in full swing with all kinds of artsy-craftsy objects for sale, including a lot of mediocre local paintings and blown-up photographs.

As we wandered around, we paused and talk to a few people who were manning their little sales stalls. Many were long-timers here, all in their sixties or seventies. All were friendly. But after a few conversations, we realized that this was not the elite, wealthy expat crowd of Boquete, just the hand to mouth crowd, most too poor to go anywhere, so they stay here year after year.

Boquete Flea Market

In any case, everybody struck us as very mellow as if they were high on grass or some tranquilizer. Overall, there was a "New Age" vibe here, where time seemed to stand still. Judging by the stalls, these people were into massage, herbs, chimes and natural supplements. Also, we encountered stalls promoting little-theater groups, reading groups, photography groups and so on. Most of these operations struck me as being run by well-meaning amateurs. At one stall featuring used books, we asked the lady if there was a real bookstore in Boquete.

"No, not at all," she replied. "A few years ago someone tried to operate one but there were not enough customers. Most get their best sellers and such from the library. If you want a real bookstore, you have to go down to David. There's a marvelous bookstore there featuring new and used books both Spanish and English."

"OK, duly noted."

More Flea Market

After that, we moved on to a stall that was promoting expat investment in Panama. There we talked to Don, a financial guy pushing Panamanian IRAs. Don was a well-groomed prosperous-looking fellow in his early 60s. He claimed his outfit, an offshore credit union based in Panama, could promise an eight percent return, the gains of which were tax-free in Panama.

"All very well, but what about paying U.S. taxes on that return." I countered.

"Well, that's between you, your tax accountant and the IRS. All I can say is that American expats living here who transferred their IRAs here and invested in CDs are very satisfied with the arrangement."

"Well, how does it work?"

"Simple. You just roll over your U.S. IRA or 401K to our credit union and we invest it in our various CDs. We can help you with the paperwork. It's a breeze. It can be done in a day or two. And you, of course, have complete control over your funds and any withdrawals you deem necessary."

Don further claimed that money was flowing in from the U.S. into his offshore credit union. "You don't even have to live here. Just show up in person, sign some papers, transfer the funds and go home."

Actually, the whole thing struck me as a tax dodge. I mean is the IRS going to check on your taxable withdrawals from an IRA or any other investment way down here in Panama? Who knows and who is going to report it? I guess the whole taxpaying thing was based on the honor system.

We spent another hour nosing around the flea market and then returned to our house around one where we decided to chill the rest of the day.

***

So here we were relaxing for what we thought would be an afternoon of splendid isolation. But when I looked out from the kitchen at the back garden who should I spy sitting on a bench right behind our bedroom window, the downstairs neighbor softly playing a flute something like Pan, the god of nature. This immediately pissed me off. What was this guy doing there? That was our back yard or so I thought until I confronted him.

"Say, would mind stopping with the flute stuff and what are you doing here anyway? I thought your turf was your downstairs apartment, the carport and the garden out front."

"Oh, didn't Howard explain. As a downstairs tenant, I have the right to make use of all the outdoor gardens including this one."

"No, he never mentioned that. I'll have a talk with him about. Anyway, I would appreciate it if you stuck to the front."

"O.K., O.K. Still let me introduce myself. No sense being neighbors without introductions.

"Sure."

We introduced ourselves. Max explained that he did free-lance high tech work for clients from around the world but he specialized in Central America and Mexico since he spoke fluent Spanish.

"So you just sit there in your shorts and sandals, and interface with the hi-tech world?"

"That's about it and I find Panama to be an excellent base from which to operate."

"Sounds great for you."

"Oh, and by the way, you might be seeing my girlfriend around here too. She stays with me in the apartment but comes and goes as she is a flight attendant on Copa Airlines. In the meantime, I'll try to keep out of your way for the week that you are here."

Softening a bit towards this guy, "Thanks. We would appreciate it. See you around."

And with that Max departed from the back garden.

And so we relaxed for the rest of the afternoon until evening and then enjoyed another tasty taco meal prepared by Yvonne and consumed as the sun went down behind the mountains.

4. COFFEE TOUR

Wednesday, May 9

The next day we were up early for our tour of a coffee plantation. There had been many to choose from. There were about four or five major coffee farms in the Boquete Valley. One even offered full hotel services. That was not for us. We wanted one small, cheap and over and done within a few hours. Thus it was that we had settled on the outfit recommended by Howard. The lady at the coffee tour desk had signed us up for Finca Dos Jefes, a small coffee farm run by a couple of American retirees.

"It's very intimate," the lady had said. "They conduct only small groups and are quite reasonable in cost. It's informative and the people who run it are very pleasant. You will learn all about the coffee growing and its processing. You will have a coffee tasting at the end of the tour and you can even grind your own coffee and take a bag home with you."

"Sounds good."

"You will really enjoy this three-hour tour."

Yvonne liked that.

"Uh, that will ninety dollars please."

***

Our tour was scheduled to begin at nine-thirty. We were to meet a representative from the coffee plantation at the tourist agency. We were there on the dot. Joining the tour with us was a single English woman. She introduced herself as Hillary. By and by, a young fellow who introduced himself as Roberto showed up in a Finca Dos Jefes van. He greeted us in fluent English and beckoned us to get into his van. We climbed aboard and were soon off. He drove along the main valley road for a couple of kilometers out of town and then turned off onto a gravel road that meandered up a mountainside for another kilometer or so until we came to the Finca Dos Jefes farm. It appeared to be a tidy little operation with a modest house, and a large coffee processing structure to the side. The grounds also had long rows of sorting tables filled with coffee beans that workers had picked and sorted by hand.

Sorting Table

Except for a couple of rows of plantings, the main crop of coffee plants was not immediately apparent. Roberto explained that they were farther up on the mountain which we would see momentarily. He told us to board a little tractor-trailer arrangement that would take us into the heart of the coffee plantation.

Soon we were off on the tractor-trailer going up a dirt track on a mountainside covered with trees, bushes and what appeared to be thick underbrush. In no way did this appear to be a cultivated coffee plantation. But as Roberto came to stop, he explained that even though it didn't look like it, this was indeed coffee country.

"You see, we find that the coffee bushes thrive best in surrounding foliage and also in the shade of larger trees. So that is why we have such irregular planting here."

And with that, he hopped off the tractor and proceeded to rifle through a nearby coffee bush and came away with a handful of green coffee beans, although not ripe. "It's a lot easier to find the beans when they are ripe because then they are bright red," he explained.

He urged us to get off the trailer and start walking around this rough hewn planting area. So we did and were soon engulfed in the foliage, much of which was hard to make our way through.

Coffee Bushes

Some of the bushes were waist high; others were towering, almost like trees. How Roberto and plantation owners kept track of all this coffee chaos was beyond me. But keep track they did and reportedly these irregular plantings yielded some of the best coffee in the Boquete valley.

Green Coffee Beans

After wandering around in the bush for a while with Roberto pointing out the characteristics of this coffee plant or that coffee plant, we returned to the tractor-trailer and climbed back on board, now taking many swigs of cold water as the day was heating up. Even in the "springtime" mountains, the days can get hot.

During our coffee excursion, we became further acquainted with Hillary from England. Her full name was Hillary Brown. I joked with Hillary that we must be distant cousins since our last name was Brown too.

As I put it: "Some of my ancestors came over from England in the mid-18th century. Forced labor they were, most were convicted thieves of one sort or another."

"Really? Maybe mine were crooks too," Hillary replied. "They just never got caught. I don't know much about my family tree although many English do."

I continued, "Yes, well it was just luck that mine made it to America even as indentured servants because a few years later due to the American Revolutionary War, they would have been shipped to Australia and I would be speaking with an Aussie accent."

She laughed. "I've been to Australia. Love the country. Maybe I will move there full time. Good weather, healthy place to live unlike England with its gloom and doom most of the year."

This made me wonder about Hillary. A very attractive woman in her early thirties I estimated. Obviously, a free spirit wandering the world. She said her day job was something in high tech and her skills were easily marketable in the English-speaking world. Indeed, a sharp, independent woman doing the world.

Soon we were back at the coffee processing shed. Roberto demonstrated how they sorted the beans, peeled, and roasted them and then bagged them for eventual sale. Of course, if you wanted to buy a bag, he would grind the beans for you on the spot. Following all of that, it was time repair to their Cafés de la Luna for a sampling of the many types of coffee the plantation produced. It was something like a wine tasting.

We were served an array of different coffee brews, around five or six, and then urged to start with the mildest cup of coffee while Roberto lectured on its attributes. We then worked our way up to the progressively stronger cups of coffee accompanied by Roberto's lecture. All very instructive but as far as I was concerned I could barely taste the differences except between the mild and the strongest. I guess I'm not a coffee connoisseur. Yvonne was much more into this than I was. She bought a little bag of ground coffee from the middle range of taste. Anyway, the coffee tasting capped our little tour of the Finca Dos Jefes. A very worthwhile and educational experience.

***

We returned to our abode for the afternoon and then towards early evening, we suited up in our tropical finest and set off for what promised to be our major dining experience in Boquete. Namely, we were going to dine at the Hotel Panamonte, an old-line resort hotel and restaurant that catered to the well-healed who wanted a bit of old-world Central American charm. This place, founded by a Swedish couple, has been around for more than 50 years. Now ranked as a landmark historical inn, it is situated at the foot of the major volcano in these parts, the Volcan Baru, known as a sleeping giant. Of course, when we arrived, due to the heavy vegetation and high-level fog, the Volcan Baru was not visible. But the hotel was in full view with its traditional rustic architecture and tin roof.

Hotel Panamonte

While the main exterior looked tropical rough with a tin roof, inside the place reeked of luxury and extended towards the back with more modern additions and upgrades. We decided that this place would work for us as we took a quick look around the lobby and discovered an alcove in the back that featured a cozy fireplace.

Alcove

It was here that I ordered a couple of margaritas for us and relaxed while Yvonne seriously studied some sort of pottery artifact.

Yvonne with Pot

Soon it was time to dine. The dining room featured a lot of elaborate window dressings, overhanging table cloths and soft chairs, something you might see anywhere in London or any other major European city. Nothing in the décor to remind you that you were indeed in Panama.

Dining Room

We were offered a small table for two near a window. The place was full so I did not protest but did mention to Yvonne that maybe we should have our meal served in the alcove with the fireplace. Yvonne told me to stop bitching. So we settled down and scanned the menu. It struck me as rather standard fare with various fish dishes, lamb and steak. I had read that the specialty here was the local trout so we ordered that with various fresh vegetable side dishes but led off the meal with a highly recommended Zapallo soup, a pumpkin soup. All of that with a chilled bottle of a local white wine.

As it turned out, the soup was excellent with Yvonne saying she could have devoured several more bowls of the Zapallo and done without the fish.

Yvonne's Pumpkin Soup

Not that the fish was that bad. Indeed, it was a fleshy yet tangy grilled trout. Normally trout is not my favorite fish dish because the average trout is rather skimpy unless you have several at once. For dessert, we had some local custard that was quite tasty and a cup of a special brand of Boquete coffee. All in all, not a bad meal. Not the greatest that we have ever had, but it did the job and it was not too expensive, somewhere around $150.00 with tip.

We topped our meal off by returning to the alcove for a while and enjoying an after-dinner cognac. And then it was back to our house with me carefully navigating the winding road up the hill in the pitch black with only our headlights to light the way. Not a streetlight in sight. End of our coffee tour and meal out day in Boquete.

Thursday, May 10

So here it was our last full day in Boquete and we had no plans at all. We considered driving up the slopes of the Volcan Baru as far as we could but I had read that you needed a four-wheel drive to get anywhere on a rutted dirt road. My all-wheel drive Pathfinder probably could have made it most of the way but with memories fresh in my head of the car rental hassles in Costa Rica, I didn't want to take any chances with this beauty. No, what we would do is further explore the lower hill country surrounding Boquete on paved roads. I could see on my tourist map of this area that there were a lot of little hotels and settlements tucked away here and there.

Around ten, we saddled up and began our explorations of some of these hillside communities. As we drove up and down the byways of these hills, we passed by various luxury houses hidden in the foliage. We stopped at one elegant looking B&B and scouted around. It had a pool out back and several cute little bungalows. It also touted the fact that it was hooked up with one of the coffee plantations nearby and offered free tours. No one was at the check-in desk but I did glance at the rate sheet. Two hundred a night with full board. In other words quite expensive for Boquete.

This aimless driving around soon got tedious so we descended into the town proper and hit the main highway again, driving out of town a few kilometers until we came upon another dedicated retirement development. This one was much more modest than the Valle Escondido. It was located on a piece of flat terrain, about ten acres I would estimate. It looked like any standard suburban development that you might find in the U.S. Namely it was laced with curvy roads with short side streets than ended in cul-de-sacs. The place looked only about a quarter built. Mostly it was vacant lots with single-family homes situated here and there. The houses were a bit more elaborate than those we had seen with the plumber at the other development.

The eerie part was the place appeared virtually empty of people until one lone, senior-looking guy came out of his house and looked around inspecting his weed-infested yard, apparently yet to be landscaped. Catching sight of us, he waved. I stopped the car, got out and greeted him.

"Looks like you're the only living person here."

"Indeed, I am alive. There are a few others here but this place is essentially deserted. Sales are slow."

He said this in a British accent so I asked him what brought him here to Panama all the way from Britain.

"Actually, I haven't lived there for quite a while. I was working for an oil company in South America. I liked the easy living in Latin America and the warm weather so my wife and I decided to retire here in Panama. As you probably know, they are very open here to retirees especially when it comes to money and investments."

"Yeah, I heard. We're giving the place a look for retirement too. The Boquete area is pleasant but I want to hit the coastal areas as well to see what that's like.

"Well, forget about Bocas del Toro on the Caribbean coast. It's full of hippies and mosquitos although the water is nice at nearby beaches. Good snorkeling and scuba diving. "

"Yeah, I had heard too about Bocas del Toro. Namely, that it was a dump full of biting sandflies."

Continuing, I said, "We are going to hit the Pacific coast towns down on the Azuero Peninsula. I hear they have great beaches and great surf as well."

"Yes, I have heard that too but this works for us. We are near to Boquete and near to David a major city in these parts with full services including good medical."

At this point, I bid him goodbye and we continued our aimless tour. At first, I had thought we might drive on to David but Yvonne protested, saying since it was noon, all she wanted to do was return to our cool abode in the hills above Boquete and relax.

And that's all we did for the rest of the day. Tomorrow we leave the paradise of Boquete.

5. AZUERO PENINSULA

Friday, May 11

We were eager to leave Boquete. I guess a do-nothing paradise wasn't for us. Good for a couple of days but after that "BORING." In any case, Howard Hilt was at our doorstep at nine sharp even though official checkout time was ten. We had a cup of coffee together on our balcony, chatted a bit and then were joined by Max from downstairs. He also worked for Howard as kind of a clean-up and maintenance man for the upstairs apartment. Maybe that's why he treated us like mere tenants in "his" apartment where he could wander around the grounds at will and I suspected hang out in the upstairs apartment when it wasn't rented out to vacationers like us.

Anyway, we bid Howard and Max a final goodbye, loaded up our luggage into the Pathfinder and were on our way out of Boquete, heading for the Azuero Peninsula and a beach town called Playa el Uverito. This was about a six-hour drive or 333 kilometers in distance.

***

Soon we arrived on the outskirts of David, as already noted, the major town in these parts. Once again we wondered if we should take a half-hour at David to check out its local resources that the expats raved about but since we had many kilometers to cover this day, we gave it only a brief glimpse as we drove through the downtown section. We could see why David was favored by expats. It had a modern hospital and a well-appointed downtown full of shops and cafes along with several well-groomed parks and fountains giving it a cooling green look.

David

For the record, David is the capital of the Chiriquí Province with a population of some 80-thousand. Checking my guide book, it turns out that it was founded in 1602 by one Francisco de Gama who derived the name from the biblical David in the bible. Religious people, what?

Moving on, we turned south onto the Pan American Highway that ran through the edge of town heading towards Panama City. Soon we were out on the countryside tooling along with Yvonne reminding me every so often to obey the speed limits of 110 k/h here which were strictly enforced or so the guidebook said. However, I didn't see a cop for the entire length of our journey. Probably off doing their Friday shopping.

As we moved along, I thought about how historic the Pan-American Highway was, all twenty-nine thousand kilometers (18,000 miles) of it. You can now drive along this highway in its various incarnations from Alaska's Arctic Circle on Prudhoe Bay down the west coast of the U.S., through Mexico, through most of Central America and South America, down to the tip of Chile. Well, maybe not quite. There is a section of Panama called the Darién Gap where the highway is almost non-existent as well as rife with disease, smugglers and criminals. For this stretch, it is recommended that you take a seagoing ferry into neighboring Colombia where you can continue your automotive journey to the bottom of the world.

After almost three hours of tedious driving, we turned off the Pan American Highway at Divisa and onto Highway 3 going south to the Azuero Peninsula. Again, there wasn't much to see because we were well inland from the Pacific Ocean, only a lot of small shanty settlements until we came to Chitre, the major city in these parts. This town struck us as kind of common and junked up, in part due to the extensive road construction that was underway. As a result, it was slow going making our way through the town and the local traffic. However, the bright spot was that we were only 48 kilometers from Las Tablas, the jumping-off point to the nearby beach town where we were going to stay, Playa el Uverito.

We plowed ahead, the drive becoming ever more scenic even though there was no sign of the ocean or even of the fact that we were on a peninsula. A glance at a map of Panama shows that the Azuero is a rather fat peninsula and continues that way as you travel south.

Azuero Peninsula

In any case, about 45 minutes later, we were on the outskirts of Las Tablas. As we made our way through the town in the now late afternoon, we noted that Las Tablas was a festive place with a lot of music going on in the parks and people milling about, some dancing, many dressed in traditional outfits. Also, judging by the facades of the buildings much of the architecture was rather charming in that traditional Central American way. This place was worth taking an in-depth look at later. But right then we had to take the turn off for our beach hotel about 15 kilometers away.

Twenty minutes later after negotiating a pothole marked road that was haphazardly paved, we arrived at Playa el Uverito. As we drove down the main drag, we passed two-story beach houses on the seaside and ratty commercial establishments on the other. Except for a brief glimpse between structures, we didn't see much beach or ocean.

By and by, on the edge of town, we came upon Hotel La Luna, a vision from a 1960s wet dream with its curvy, spiral stairway up to the second floor. In front, a big kidney-shaped pool beckoned with appropriate foliage planted here and there. All in all, a very pleasing sight.

Hotel La Luna

We pulled into the parking lot adjacent to the hotel and no sooner got out of our car than were met by an enthusiastic proprietor, a tall bearded dude. He introduced himself as Luca from Milan.

"Milan, Italy?"

"Yes, but it was so many years ago that I emigrated from there that I now feel more Panamanian. But enough talk. Let me show you to your room."

And with that, he grabbed Yvonne's rolly suitcase, dragging it over the gravel and I followed close behind with my own suitcase. Up the spiral staircase, we went with Luca treating Yvonne's suitcase as mere handbag while I struggled to drag my suitcase, bumpity-bump, up the stairs.

Our room was simple and spare with a double bed and what looked like an original painting on one wall. Kind of expressionistic. Good enough. We also noticed other paintings on the wall of the balcony and then later downstairs in a small cramped lobby and breakfast room. We found out later that all the paintings were the work of Luca Laghetti, our Italian host.

After we got settled, we asked Luca for a restaurant recommendation. He nodded to a restaurant across the street.

"It's nice with a view of the beach of the ocean beyond. It might be a bit crowded this evening though being Friday night. Very popular."

Hungry and not wanting to search around, we walked over to Rincon Del Faro and Luca was right. It was crowded but we managed to get a table for two on the balcony overlooking their big swimming pool and beyond a dark, gray beach and the wide Pacific. The food was O.K. We had fish tacos or something like it with a couple of large beers. But it was not a peaceful dining experience for next to us was a large noisy family gathering consisting of at least eight kids and two sets of parents and grandparents all talking and laughing in loud voices. One of the apparent grandparents, a well-groomed macho type dominated the chattering chaos by bossing the kids and everyone else around. All the time Yvonne and I were thinking, don't these Latin American types know how to be low key and quiet? Apparently not.

After dinner, we walked back to La Luna and bedded down for the night, tired from our long journey from the cool mountains of Boquete to the steamy shores of Playa el Uverito.

Saturday, May 12

We were up bright and early the next morning ready to see what Playa el Uverito had to offer. First, we hiked over to the town beach. What we saw was a far cry from the powder white beaches we had seen in Antonio Park, Costa Rica. It was a heavy gray sand beach, not at all groomed with a lot of rivulets cutting their way into the sand and forming little inland pools. The ocean itself was also dull gray with small dirty waves. About the only thing inviting here was the water temperature somewhere in the 80s that we felt while wading out knee-deep. But after this little dip, all thoughts of going swimming in this fetid looking ocean instantly vanished.

Playa el Uverito

After our short beach excursion, we went back to the Pathfinder and started driving south out of town to check out the beachfront real estate offerings. And there they were one after the other cheek by jowl, one oversized residence after another on the oceanside and on the land side, less crammed in but still plentiful. I thought further proof that the Panamanians must like living close to their neighbors because I couldn't imagine foreigners buying into a beach town like this.

After an hour or so of this minor exploration, we returned to La Luna for an early lunch and a swim in the pool before venturing out again. During this time, we ran into Luca tending to his landscaping.

"So how do you like our little village?" he asked.

"It's O.K. but the beach isn't much, is it? Kind of rudimentary," I replied. "I also saw a sign in both Spanish and English warning of riptides."

"Yes, rip-tides there are. In general, improvements are always promised but never seem to happen. The beaches are far better down the peninsula around Pedasi and even farther south, there are good surfing beaches."

"Yes, so I have heard but we don't have time to go down there. As you know we check out tomorrow."

"Yes, alas, there is a lot to see around here."

"Seems like much of it is for sale."

"Yes it is but much of it is an illusion," said Lucas.

"Oh, how so?"

"Developers come in and buy several lots. I personally know one such developer who bought six lots and built an oceanfront house of his own on one of the lots."

Luca went on to explain that the idea was to use such a house as bait for friends and other potential investors who then buy their own lots and build their own houses on speculation believing that the cash value of their houses will surely rise for a later sale because the Panama realtors have declared the area up and coming but that in reality nothing much has changed in the market.

"Most of these realtors have never even visited the area," declared Luca.

After this conversation at poolside and a beer, and a few lunchables leftover from Luca's generous breakfast, we got dressed again and headed out. This time to search the environs of Las Tablas.

First, we drove around the outskirts of Las Tablas to take a look at the real estate offerings. And sure enough, there they were, one good-looking house after another though not mansions by any stretch but still nice looking one-story ranches or bungalows in the Hispanic style. According to the info sheets in the boxes out front all had three bedrooms and two baths with full landscaping, all going for $150K and up. Overall, we felt they were much better buys for a retiree than paying top dollar in Boquete.

However, when we got out of our air-conditioned car, the wet blanket heat hit us and we wondered how many had swimming pools which we would consider essential in this climate. We debated checking in at a local real estate office but decided not to. Yvonne didn't want to listen to a sales pitch from some hustling realtor. While we didn't go inside any of these homes for sale, we did notice on the info sheets that all had air-conditioning.

Las Tablas House

Las Tablas Plaza

After an hour or so of wandering around on the outskirts, we headed into downtown Las Tablas to see what was what. Essentially, we saw exactly what we saw yesterday plus some interesting side streets. Here and there, we saw gringo retiree types going about their daily shopping.

We also drove by restaurant advertising a full-scale Sunday brunch buffet with giant margaritas. Hmm. Maybe that was for us tomorrow before leaving the area. Overall, Las Tablas appeared to be a charming town and not too touristy like Boquete.

We headed back to Playa el Uverito, took another swim in the pool and then before going out to dinner again, we let Luca show us his expressionist paintings, maybe hoping for a sale.

Luca's Art

His art was interesting, but we were in no mood to buy anything. We thanked him for showing us his wares and then we walked over to the Rincon Del Faro across the street, this time snagging a table far away from the crowd and dined on a whole fried Corvina fish, something like sea bass, that of course along with a couple of margaritas. After dinner, we walked along the beach briefly in the twilight and then retired to La Luna. That was it for the day. Tomorrow we are out of here.

Sunday, May 13

The next morning we packed up, bid Luca goodbye and set off for Las Tablas and our Sunday brunch with visions of morning margaritas dancing in our heads. When we arrived at El Caseron around ten, the place was jammed with gringos. We managed to get a small table that looked out on a patio which itself was full. Still, our waiter was prompt and stood by to take our drink order before we headed to the buffet. I was all set to order a couple of margaritas but Yvonne intervened saying, "Allan, you have to drive a long way today back to Panama City on an unfamiliar road."

"Yes, that is true. But I can hold my liquor especially if we hang around for an hour here. I promise to have only one."

"Well, I would feel a lot better if you only had a beer instead," she insisted. "That would probably go better with the buffet based on what I have seen."

So to keep the peace, I ordered two Balboa beers for us. Once that detail was taken care of, we headed over to the buffet hot table and examined the offerings and they were vast indeed.

Shall I list them? Yes, of course. First, scrambled eggs mixed with green peppers or fried eggs if you wish. Then there was bacon, sausage, roast potatoes, grilled giant mushrooms, grilled tomatoes, fried eggplant, tiny enchiladas filled with ground-up sausage and cheese. Pasta if you wanted it and no dearth of seafood with piles of grilled shrimp, fried calamari and chunks of Covina. Also loads of fruit and salad offerings too numerous to mention.

Needless to say, we filled our plates and went to work. I quickly downed my Balboa as I fed my face and then unable to resist, I ordered another telling Yvonne that any alcoholic content would be immediately defused by a lot of the food in my belly. That was true by the fact that we would spend over an hour devouring our buffet goodies.

Finally, a little after eleven, we called it quits and waddled back to our Pathfinder, hopeful that this repast would replace lunch and maybe even dinner.

Around 11:30, we were out on Highway 3 heading back to Chitre. Once again, we had to navigate the construction mess in and around Chitre. That slowed us down but we soon arrived at the intersection of Highway 3 and the Pan American highway. From here, it was a straight shot back to Panama City some 218 kilometers, about three hours away. I was all for going nonstop to our destination but Yvonne urged me to turn off at Coronado, a supposed luxury development on the oceanfront about 90 kilometers from Panama City.

"What's your hurry?" she asked. "I thought we were here to check out the retirement offerings. Coronado is supposed to be one of the best places."

"Yes," I replied, "but based on what I have seen so far, the Pacific oceanfront in Panama leaves a lot to be desired."

"Oh, party pooper. Just a little peek. It's right on the way. Fodor's says it's a great little spot."

Yvonne was right. We did have time to spare. Anyway, our reservation was secured at where we were going to stay in Panama City, the Country Inn and Suites near the canal.

So we turned off at Coronado to examine its offerings. After driving along the main oceanfront boulevard, which was lined with shops, all we saw were mega-condo buildings, many blocking out the beachfront and another gray sand beach where you could see it. It seemed like most of the beaches had been privatized by the condo dudes. However, we did stop at one little beachfront park open to the public and snapped some photos.

Coronado Beach

Yvonne & Beach

Only after returning to the Pathfinder, did we notice a sign in faded Spanish and English warning about crime on the beaches and possible riptides. I guess by the deserted look of the beach, most residents stuck to their condo swimming pools all nice and secure in their upscale condos.

One of the major selling points for Coronado is that it's a "short" drive to Panama City with all its urban attractions. Actually, it's a little over an hour's drive. All duly noted but we did not find the area especially attractive. More like South Florida.

Coronado Condo

So we ended our retirement hunting for the day and as it turned out for the rest of the trip. And we headed off for Panama City or rather the Canal Zone in Panama City where our hotel was located. This was a straight shot on a four-lane expressway through a mountainous area. We crossed the iconic Bridge of the Americas and then voila, we were soon in a park-like area on the waterfront near the canal and there located amidst tropical splendor and near the Amador Causeway was our hotel, the Country Inn and Suites waiting for us. (Now called the Radisson.)

We parked and lugged our suitcases into the large open-air lobby and were immediately struck about how plush this place was. A glance out the back revealed a couple of large, elegantly shaped pools and an extensive patio area with plenty of lounging chairs about. Of course, an outdoor bar was nearby.

Country Inn & Suites

Even though it was late afternoon, I wanted to immediately plunge into one of the pools to get the road dirt off me and finally have my gigantic margarita. We did just that right after we checked in. We both hit the pool and I had my margarita. Later, we dined at a TGI Friday's next door which had yielded to Panamanian cuisine but still served old-fashioned American hamburgers. An hour later back in our luxurious room with a big king size bed, we both zonked out in a matter of minutes.

All in all, it had been quite a day for us traveling from Playa el Uverito to Las Tablas to Coronado to here. We got a pretty good glimpse of what Panama's Pacific beachfront had to offer. But standby, there was still a lot more to come. One more day in Panama City and then we would be off to the San Blas Islands on the Caribbean side of Panama.

6. SAN BLAS ISLANDS

Tuesday, May 15

Early Tuesday morning, we drove to the Gelabert Airport a few kilometers away. This was the main airport for all the flights to the San Blas region. We said goodbye to our Pathfinder checking it in and parking it in the local Hertz parking lot. The idea was we would not need a rental car for the one day we would still be in Panama City before flying back to the States. Yes, this mad dash around Central America would soon be coming to an end. But first, we had to experience out-island life in the San Blas Archipelago.

First up, we had to check-in at Panama Air. An attractive young lady behind the check-in counter was examining her nails as we approached. She reluctantly took a break from her nails and duly checked us in. Done with that she nodded to a big burly male attendant who stepped up and hefted our luggage onto the scale and then onto the ramp belt. The lady behind the counter didn't miss a beat and continued to examine her nails and then pat her hair.

I had noticed a similar pattern among all the young female attendants both at this airport and then later when we flew out of the major Panama airport, the Tocumen International Airport. All were nice looking and nicely made up. But all emanated an attitude that they were doing you, the passenger, a favor by simply being on duty. I figured most were hired through one family connection or another.

Our flight left right on schedule at 8 a.m. We were aboard a small passenger plane that could carry forty passengers but today only twenty of us were flying. I remember it was a Fokker 100, a turboprop plane designed for short hauls. We flew for about a half-hour, halfway to our destination, but then the pilot announced the plane was having engine trouble and that we would have to turn back and land back at Gelabert. We passengers were visibly upset at this prospect because maybe this crate couldn't make it back to our point of origin and maybe it would be better to land at the first available airport. But being over what appeared to be dense jungle, that was not an option. The other thing bugging us was that we might lose a full day in the San Blas because of this shoddy aircraft. And sure enough, as soon as we landed at Gelabert, (thank God!), the pilot announced they would take a few hours to procure another plane and we would be on our way again.

Well, it took more than three hours to get another plane. It was past noon when we took off for the hour flight. Half the day was shot. However, this flight was smooth and we did get a good look at a lot of jungle. Checking my map, I saw that we had been skirting the remote and inaccessible Darién Province. I could imagine all the bleached bones of the Spanish explorers who perished down there centuries ago.

We finally landed at the Playon Chico Airport which served many of the islands in the San Blas Archipelago. However, as important as it was to the region, it had only a dirt runway and a shanty shed for a terminal. Four other couples got off with us, apparently headed to the same resort as we were, namely the Yandup Island Lodge.

Once off the plane, we were greeted by a resort representative a sharp-looking Kuna Indian dude in shorts and a T-shirt. He introduced himself as Carlos and then led us over to a dock on the bay where motioned for us to board a small motor launch, which would take us to the island of Yandup. The luggage would go in another boat. As we set off, we got a glimpse of the town of Playon Chico about a half-mile away over a causeway. It appeared to be nothing more than shacks on pylons over the water.

Playon Chico Village

Chugging along the placid bay, we soon spotted Yandup Island. From a distance, it appeared to be a typical flat tropical island with stands of waving palm trees and a number of outbuildings. As we drew closer, we could see a collection of resort-type dwellings, namely bungalows built over the water and the main building that was presumably a restaurant and a social center.

By and by, we docked at a rather shaky resort pier. We then disembarked and were immediately met by the island staff, all indigenous Kuna Indians except for one lone white woman who was in charge.

"Come on up to the welcome center, and we will check you all in," she announced. "By the way my name is Carol. And don't worry about your luggage. My staff will distribute it later to the bungalows you are staying in." Carol looked and acted like a Sergeant at Arms, definitely calling the shots.

We duly followed her up to the welcome center where a couple of Kunas who spoke excellent English checked us in.

Our bungalow was located on the other side of the small island about 100 yards away in a grove of palm trees. When I made the original reservations for this place, I decided to forego the bungalow over the water thing since it cost a lot more than what I was paying, about 200-dollars a day including meals.

At first, glance when we entered our bungalow, it seemed charming with a veranda and view of the bay out back. It was an all-thatch affair made out of local materials. Inside was a double bed under mosquito netting, a couple of chairs, a small table and a rather primitive looking bathroom off to the side with a sea-water shower. We had been told there was only intermittent solar-powered electricity and no potable drinking water. Of course no air-conditioning but a large overhead fan for cooling. In other words, rustic. A kind of back to nature thing. Or as they say in the brochures, an eco-resort true to its native roots. Still, that was we supposedly wanted—a close to nature experience with the Kuna Indians.

Yandup Island Bungalow

Once settled in our bungalow, we took a short tour around the resort. First, we walked over to a little beach that we assumed was the main swimming area for the guests. It looked decent with fine white sand and crystal clear waters. Just offshore, I spotted a few coral heads that looked intriguing. Moving on, we hiked over to the welcome center and restaurant which was of course built over the water. I briefly wondered if it would survive a hurricane or even a strong tropical storm. Charming but kind of flimsy.

(By the way, Panamanians claim that Panama has never been hit by a hurricane because of its geographical configuration of being situated on an isthmus and being too far south of the hurricane track.)

Dining Room

Once our self-tour was done, we headed back to our bungalow and put on our bathing suits for a late afternoon swim. By the way, the heat was still humid and stifling and the water only slightly cooler. Yvonne waded around for a while on the sandy portion of the swimming hole while I swam out with my snorkeling gear and explored several little coral heads. Charming but hardly spectacular even with a few damsel fishies darting around. Soon back on the beach lounging in recliners, I ordered a beer from a Kuna lad, a beach boy who had been hanging around. He came back in a flash and soon all was good. After an hour or so, we returned to our bungalow. I took a warm salt-water shower, followed by a bucket of freshwater, dressed and then around six we went over to the restaurant for a drink and dinner.

Four or five other couples were already at the bar and in the restaurant when we got there. We ordered a couple of beers and sat down at a vacant table but no sooner than we had gotten settled than a heavyset woman from a nearby table started talking to us in a loud voice with the standard observations and questions:

"Isn't this place wonderful? So isolated authentic. We came yesterday and are amazed by how well it is run by these Indians."

"Really?"

"Well, yes. You, know of course that a Kuna family owns this place and that all the money they make goes for employment of the locals and aid to that village you saw coming in….." She paused to catch her breath.

Meanwhile, the husband just sat there silently sipping his beer and looking out over the water. This woman reminded me of the actress Shelly Winters in one of her blabbermouth roles.

She continued. She introduced herself and the fact that they were from Texas. (Big surprise.) We respond with minimum information. "Browns from Chicago…Yes, first time here. Yes, yes, very pleasant here. A little paradise."

Finally, we were approached by a waiter. He announced the menu for the evening. A common menu for all—fish, rice, plantains, fresh vegetables. For desert a flan of some sort. What kind of fish I asked. He shrugged, simply saying delicious fish fresh caught this morning right from this bay. I let it go. It probably didn't matter.

We settled back and gazed out over the water in the now twilight sky. The Texas couple had eaten and gone. Good. Soon our meal arrived. We ordered a couple of beers to go with it.

The meal was well cooked and quite tasty. The grilled fish was suburb. I suspected that it was a sea bass that we had earlier in our trip, Covina wasn't it?

After dinner, we hung around for a while talking to another couple from New York. Much quieter than the Texans. We briefly compared notes as to our urban existence and eventually bid them good night, returning to our thatched hut. As we entered, we noticed that the lights were on and our bed had been turned down and the mosquito netting was all nicely arranged over our bed.

We undressed for bed, tired from the day's travel. Yvonne went to sleep immediately while I read for a while. Then I turned out the lights. Suddenly all was dark and the night noises started out, a buzzing chorus of insects. I could imagine them crawling around the cabin. Then I heard a mosquito buzzing about outside the curtain. I was glad that I had taken my Malarone pill for malaria which was said to be around these parts. Soon I dropped off to sleep. Day one in paradise over and out.

Wed. May 16

After a fulsome breakfast of eggs, sausage, mangos and several other tropical goodies along with some great local coffee, we sat back and pondered the day's schedule.

Checking the event blackboard, we discovered that the main and only event was a hiking tour into the jungle on the mainland. The stated reason was to visit a Kuna cemetery on a hilltop about an hour hike into the jungle with guides explaining all about the flora and fauna of the jungle on the way. This did not sound like a very inspiring idea to me sweating it out in a mosquito-ridden jungle but Yvonne was all for it. No, what I wanted to do was to lounge around my thatched hut, read, and snorkel on the little beach and in general goof off for the day. So Yvonne went off with the group after telling me that I would be sorry. In fact, I broke up my day of leisure by renting a kayak and paddling around the island for a workout rather than being an entire slug for the entire day. By and by, Yvonne returned, all sweating and exhausted and full of bug bites. (Did you take your Malarone, dear?) Nevertheless, she said she was glad she went on it.

Kuna Cemetery

"A very interesting cemetery with a lot of the Kuna culture," she explained. "We are lucky the Kunas around here are somewhat unspoiled."

"I suppose," I replied, "but I read in the guidebook that while they are semi-autonomous in Panama, their way of life is still being threatened. From what I infer is that the 21st century is making a lot of inroads into Kuna land. Take this whole tourist eco thing. To me, it slightly smells like a racket. Sort of pseudo primitive living at a price."

"Oh, Allan, you are being a cynic. I don't deny that but let's enjoy what they're offering now."

"Right now what this place is offering is a lot of sand flies," I replied. "Have you noticed them? At first, you don't but later you are covered in bumps."

"Yes, I have. Let's get off this beach and return to our little hut," said Yvonne as started back to our abode.

And that was about it for day two in Paradise. Dinner was also similar to the night before with the only difference being a different kind of fish. Meanwhile, some new faces had shown up making it easy to ignore the loud-mouth Texas lady as she accosted a new couple at the resort. Also, there was one lone middle-aged but well-preserved woman on board. While polished and charming, she quietly told us she was from a large travel agency checking out the place to see if they could recommend it to their clients. More about her later.

Thursday, May 17

This was the day for a snorkeling and island exploration trip. Let me explain about these trips. When I read the web site for this place, they listed all these fabulous daily excursions you could go on giving you the impression that you would have a lot to choose from each day. But that was not the case at least when we were there. It really boiled down to one excursion each day, take it or leave it. Well, this day Yvonne and I signed up for this excursion because it was the main reason we were here: to snorkel crystal blue waters and see an interesting island or two. (Actually, there were 365 islands in the San Blas archipelago of which only 49 were inhabited, all billed as coral islands) Now I have seen real coral islands in the South Pacific, namely the atolls in French Polynesia and have likewise snorkeled them and even scuba dived on the surrounding reefs. I was expecting something like that, albeit with a Caribbean twist, probably with more vegetation than on a South Pacific atoll.

San Blas Motu

Thus it was with high expectations that we set off with three other couples in a motor launch and picnic lunches for a day on the small islands. About the only downside was the loudmouth lady from Texas and her quiet husband was one of the couples. She was going on about how she was looking forward to snorkeling, something she had never done before but also allowed that she was a strong swimmer and thus would catch on quickly.

So off we chugged for about a half-hour across the placid bay on a beautiful day with clear skies and relatively low humidity. Soon we arrived at our first little island or "motu" as some call it. It had an inviting white sand beach fringed with palm trees. The guide/boat boy claimed it had great coral ridges surrounding it and abundant fish life just offshore in depths ranging from five to ten feet. Perfect for snorkeling.

He cut the engine about fifty yards offshore and encouraged us to gear up with masks snorkels and fins. Now, of these three couples only we, Yvonne and I, had brought our own gear. Admittedly, it had been a pain lugging mask, fins, and snorkel along in our luggage but when we slipped on our customized gear without a hassle, it was well worth it.

The other couples were using resort supplied gear and struggled to get it on with a lot of on-the-spot adjustment. The Texas lady was having an especially hard time. Her husband, who usually didn't say much, threw down his gear and said, "Fuck it. I'll just wade around. You go ahead honey and enjoy yourself."

After a struggle, the Texas lady did manage to get her gear on straight thanks to the help of the guide/boat boy and went over the side with the rest of us, creating a small tidal wave. Right then we were in about eight feet of water, too deep for the novice snorkelers, so I took charge and led the group over twenty yards or so into shallow five feet water. Here they could put their feet down on the sand bottom and feel secure. However, the boat boy had warned us not to step on the coral and damage it. "Stand on the sand," he yelled.

In the meantime, while the others got used to snorkeling about in the shallow water, I snorkeled my way over to the deeper water, all the time peering down through my mask. And yes, there it was one little coral canyon after another still pristine and full of fish life. At various points, I dove down eight feet or so for a closer look at the coral and fish life and was immediately engulfed in swarms of black and yellow damsel fish. Once the swarm abated, I spotted a slow-moving rainbow parrot fish skirting the bottom, feeding on coral and then shitting it out as fine as sand farther on. On another dive, I spotted a small nursing shark resting in a crevice under a coral outcropping and then a stingray nestling in the sand, expertly disguised. After about twenty minutes of this, I finned my way back to the others and hooked up with Yvonne who was snorkeling around in the shallow water, marveling at the fish life surrounding even the small corals.

By this time, the other couple had ventured farther out into the depths and were finally getting the hang of snorkeling. Only Yvonne and Texas lady were left in the shallows standing firmly on the bottom. At one point, the Texas lady ripped off her mask and declared that this snorkeling was a waste of time. She hadn't really snorkeled at all because her mask kept leaking. Then seeing me back, she wadded over and pleaded with me to give her some snorkeling tips. I yielded and gave her a short snorkeling lesson, namely demonstrating how to put the mask on so it wouldn't leak, how to adjust the snorkel for easy breathing while your head was submerged and then I finned around showing how easy it was to fin and control your direction, etc.

She gamely imitated me and did rather well, even breathing controllably through the snorkel. She finally overcame her fears and started to marvel at the little corals and fish life in the shallow water. After ten minutes or so of doing this, she asked me to take her out into the deeper waters so she could get a look at the larger coral heads there.

At this point Yvonne was feeling more comfortable snorkeling so she wanted to come too. So I dutifully led them out twenty yards of so, and there we began to see the coral canyons. The Texas lady did O.K. for a while but at one point, she tried to dive down a few feet like I was doing but met with disaster. She came up choking and sputtering, her snorkel and her mask askew. As she tread water, she declared, she had had enough and wanted to go back to the shallow area.

Meanwhile, Yvonne had gotten the knack of deep water snorkeling and was having a grand old time cruising around marveling at the underwater sights. Nonetheless, I rounded her up and then led them both back to the shallow water, our snorkeling expedition basically over.

At this point, I was curious about the motu itself shimmering seductively off in the distance. The last time I explored an island like this was a motu inside the Bora Bora reef. And while I didn't expect a duplicate, I did expect similarities. Here is what I wrote then:

> *I headed inland passing through a stand of coconut palms to a grassy clearing. Here away from the trade winds, the temperature jumped a good ten degrees. I started sweating and flies buzzed around my head. I checked my watch: 2:30 p.m. The afternoon doldrums were closing in. Time for a nap. I shook off my drowsiness and tramped on through to the other side of the motu. I sat for a while on a narrow beach admiring the view of Bora-Bora and then followed the beach until it disappeared into a jumble of coral debris.*
>
> *Cutting back into the interior, I gingerly picked my way through a wall of thick underbrush, trying to avoid any crawly things that might be lurking about. Eventually, I emerged from the brush on the other side of the island and plunged into the lagoon to cool off.*
>
> *So this was motu life, the stuff of South Seas legend. I wondered how long anyone could live on such an island before the reality sank in. This was nothing more than a small sand spit topped by palm trees and infested with flies. The views were great but any stay longer than a three-hour picnic would drive most Westerners nuts.*

Well to make a long story short, Yvonne and I did wade ashore and onto the white sand beach. We rested for a few minutes while the boat boy with his picnic supplies set up lunch. With more minutes to kill, we took a short hike into the interior of this little island and yes, once you got through the palm fringe, there were a few grassy areas but most of the interior was underbrush. Nonetheless, we forged ahead. (For the record, we were not barefoot but wearing the little rubber booties that inserted into our fins.)

Soon we came out to the other side onto a rocky beach and rougher water. A typical configuration for these islets. We then hiked back, joined the others and enjoyed a picnic lunch that featured cold barbequed chicken and potato salad, washed down with beer.

After lunch, we climbed back on board the launch and the

guide/boat boy gave us a choice. We could go to another snorkeling spot or zoom around and explore other islets, one of which featured a small Kuna Village. I wanted another snorkeling spot but I was out-voted by the others, so I figured no big loss and settled back to enjoy the ride. As it turned out all the islets were pretty much the same and the village was nothing special, just another ramshackle collection of shacks.

We docked at the small Kuna Village briefly, looked around but the small settlement appeared to be deserted or maybe everybody was taking a siesta. In any case, we didn't stay long and then headed back to the resort, arriving around 2 p.m. And that was it for the outing, our day of exploration and snorkeling.

***

That evening, we dined with the travel agent and discussed her take on Yandup Lodge.

"So what do you think?" I asked. "Are you going to recommend this place to your clients?"

"Well, that depends," she replied. "There are a lot of pluses here but also quite a few negatives. I have to come clean with my clients on all of that."

"So what are the pluses and minuses?" I persisted.

"Well, at first sight, it is a gorgeous tropical setting with what appears to be charming thatched huts both on land and on over the water. It's hard to beat that setting—a small tropical islet with waving palm trees and a nice white sand beach. The basic price of around $200 to $250 a day is somewhat reasonable for what you get at an all-inclusive resort, meals, tours, cheap drinks. It certainly looks like a good place to relax in a hammock and gaze out over the tropical bay."

"So what are the negatives?"

"The main one is possible boredom. I wouldn't advise staying here more than three nights or the average American might be bored. And the food they serve while fairly well done, it is always the same every meal. Fish, fish, fish, sometimes chicken, plantains, rice, etc. It gets monotonous fast. Then there are a lot of little things like the skimpy towels they provide, no beach towels at all. And all the bugs at night. No way to keep them out of those leaky thatched huts. Of course, no air-conditioning. Thank God for the mosquito netting. Even the over-the-water cabins still have bugs and at least this time of year no breezes."

She paused taking a sip of her margarita. "Then there is the question of the all-Kuna staff. They are very nice and aim to please but they are just not professional. And their English is barely passable. Have you noticed that after nine at night, there is no staff about, not even the manager Carol? They all return to the mainland and their village. Nobody is in charge here overnight. And most importantly, there is no nighttime security here. While somewhat remote, there is crime in the San Blas Islands. Tourists are constantly being ripped off of their belongings when they leave for the day's excursions. There are also reports of nighttime assaults. Add to that, rumors of heavy drug trafficking in this area and threats of kidnapping. I could go on but is that enough for you?"

"Oh, yeah, we were already aware of some of the issues. Still, would you recommend it?"

"Yes, with qualifications. The odds are minuscule that something serious would happen to a tourist staying here. Probably the most annoying thing is the sand fly infestation. The people who run this place should do something about that."

"Hear, hear."

"Also annoying are the little extra charges for drinks, use of kayaks, etc. Nickle and dime stuff. On the question of excursions, their advertising is misleading."

"Yeah, I have noticed that," I agreed. "They imply that there are many excursions to choose from daily when in fact, there is only one a day. You have no choice. You either go on it or sit on the islet."

She interjected, "But enough critiquing, I'm flying to Boca Del Torres on the northern Caribbean coast tomorrow to check that out."

"Well, we hear it's good there too but not an island experience," I replied.

"We'll see. It seems to be very popular among the younger set. In any case, there is a four-star hotel there that I will be staying at."

And that ended our conversation about the Yandup Island Lodge.

Friday, May 18

Playon Chico

The next morning, before we flew out, Carlos took us on a tour of Playon Chico. It turned out to be a picturesque third world dump of thatched houses. Most had dirt floors, no indoor plumbing and spotty electricity. The inhabitants slept in hammocks slung in the interior of the huts. Although we did notice a few concrete houses for the prosperous few. And of course, there were mobs of kids running about. Carlos told us that the average Kuna family had seven children.

Carlos & Kids

While his kids were cute and well cared for, a lot of the kids here appeared to us to be inbred with quite a few albinos. We wondered what the Panamanian government was doing to help the Kunas out other than supplying them with churches and the word of God because we noted three major churches in this small enclave—a Catholic church, a Baptist church and a Church of the Latter Day Saints, i.e. a Mormon church. While wandering around the village, we ran into a couple of young blonde Americans on a basketball court, teaching the kids to play basketball. When they saw us, they disappeared into the shadows of huts. Carlos said they were probably Mormon missionaries bringing the word of God. What? Via basketball?

Despite the poverty, the Kunas appeared to have a rich living culture based their colorful weavings and carvings that we saw on sale. Of course, Yvonne bought a small colorful throw rug known as a Kuna "mola."

Satellite TV Dish

Walking around, we also saw several satellite TV dishes with jerry-rig hook-ups to electric generators. And as we made our way over to the airport, we spotted a nice looking school with kids running around in little uniforms—white shirts, blouses and navy blue shorts. The Kunas apparently valued education. But at the same time we had noted another group of Kuna kids in the village checking each other's head for lice.

While waiting for our plane to arrive, I ruminated on the past few days in Kuna land. Supposedly, the Yandup resort was run by and for the Kunas but at two hundred plus dollars a day, I wondered where the money was actually going. Certainly not to the Kunas based on what we had seen in this village.

Also, I noticed a Panamanian military presence near the airport. Carlos had told us that they functioned as border police. Their main job was intercepting drugs as well as policing the community.

As noted earlier, on paper, the Kunas are a self-governing, independent enclave of Panama but really, they are dependent on the Panamanian economy. A local English teacher on the flight in told us that many Kunas leave for Panama City where they work at various menial jobs or maybe produce and sell their art and crafts. Few return permanently. So the question is "wither goest the Kunas?" Who knows?

In any case, here's a review of the Yandup Kuna resort I wrote for Trip Advisor:

A one-star resort at four-star prices. If you want to live like a Kuna Indian in a thatched hut in stifling humidity with no air conditioning, only slow moving fans, dim lighting and barely any water, saltwater at that, then the Yandup Resort in the San Blas islands is the place for you. What it does offer is a very friendly and competent Kuna staff that aims to please, good food (although not enough of it) and fairly decent snorkeling on the little out-islands. It is definitely a place to get away from it all because there is no cell phone service, no Wi-Fi, no television, just the sound of the waves and the rustle of the palms. Bring a couple of good books, a flashlight and lots of strong bug repellent because the sand flies (no-see-ums) are ferocious. Recommend a two or three-night stay only. Any longer than that, you might be eaten alive.

The flight back to Panama City went off without incident or delay but we did stop at two other island destinations in the San Blas to pick up passengers, thus giving us an overall look at the archipelago. Certainly picturesque from the air and probably meeting all the criteria for a tropical paradise, but probably slated for mega-development in the near future. We will see.

Saturday, May 19

Done with the San Blas, we were now back at our luxury hotel, the Country Inn and Suites near the canal for another full day before leaving. We had no real plans for the day except to lounge to work on our tans at poolside. Both Yvonne and I were getting dark. Still, I wondered if even with sunblock, was this good for our skin now that we were both so-called senior citizens, i.e. over 65? But hey, you only live once.

Finally tiring of poolside lounging, I went on a little hike around the causeway park which was extensive. Of course, I picked the wrong time of day to do this—early afternoon with the sun at its blazing hottest and with high humidity. I finally took refuge on a bench in the shade overlooking the approaches to the canal.

As I did so, I began to ponder the significance of our sojourn through Costa Rica and Panama. Noting the constant hot and heavy humid air here, I realized that it never really changes. It is always this way for the entire year except for rain now and then. I could see how living here year-round could become boring and uncomfortable if you were used to seasons. Already I was yearning for a crisp fall day or better yet snowy mountains with a lot of downhill skiing. Of course, one could always fly back to the states to get a taste of winter and mountains. I knew that Floridians did that all the time. They were among the most enthusiastic skiers in the Rockies.

To be fair, there were a lot of positives about Panama that made it more attractive to me than Costa Rica. First of all, the currency is based on the American dollar. You can use U.S. currency here. No worries about currency exchange rates. Second, Panama City is a happening place. The downtown is full of new skyscrapers, mostly banks. It looks and feels like Miami. Money was flooding in from Europe and the US, all in an effort to escape from what some believe will be the financial Armageddon of the Western World.

Then there was the attraction of free health care for anyone including foreign retirees living here. And believe it or not, when it comes to looking after your health, Panama City has a John Hopkins Hospital, supposedly state of the art and with John Hopkins trained doctors. They say they can do anything, they do in the states. I already mentioned the high praise of the medical facilities in David. Of course, living here meant kissing off Medicare coverage which does not extend overseas outside of a few U.S. possessions like the U.S. Virgin Islands.

And then there was the prospect of relatively cheap living here. No taxes on foreigners I heard but you still owed those taxes in the U.S. And as also noted, to live like an American back home in similar housing, this place was no real bargain. Would we be happy in a small two-bedroom, one-bath bungalow like we saw in Boquete? Probably not.

With all of this churning in my head, I returned to the hotel and hashed some of this out with Yvonne in our nice air-conditioned room. Ultimately, we realized that Costa Rica and Panama were not an option for us. Oh, it was seductive with its tropical setting and air-conditioned mountain towns and relatively cheap living but really, not for us.

We polished off the day off with dinner in the nearby old city, Casco Viejo. For some reason, the old city looked even more charming than before. Maybe it was because in the early evening it was all lit up with festival lights. Anyway, we dined at a quaint little restaurant that we had spotted from our earlier tour that served all the traditional Panamanian cuisine, i.e. chicken, rice, plantains, etc. That along with a couple of Balboa Beers satisfied our hunger and provided a fitting end to our sojourn in Central America.

Sunday, May 20

We flew home the next day without delay and incident, returning to a Chicago spring all tanned and rested. After a few weeks though, we were getting restless wondering where to go next on this never-ending quest for a perfect retirement spot.

Hasta Luego

PART III: CHILE

PREFACE

So here it was three years later (2015) after our trek down to Central America to check out retirement possibilities. By now we had decided on our retirement spot--Pueblo, Colorado. Its attractions were many—relatively high altitude (4800 ft.), close to skiing in the Southern Rockies, 300-days of sunshine, and cheap living.

For about 350K in 2014, you could have a mini-mansion with stunning views of Pike's Peak and the Wetmore Mountains. Also, it was far less crowded than the Front Range north of Denver. Plenty of open space. But the primary reason we moved here was that our physician daughter Vanessa lived there for a time. When she left, we bought her barely used new house.

Anyway, once settled in, we began to scope out new travel possibilities. One of them was a trip to Chile at the bottom of the Southern Hemisphere. This was at the instigation of Vanessa who had signed up for a week-long hiking trek to explore Patagonia by starting from the Chilean side and working its way across to Argentina.

This trip intrigued both Yvonne and I. Not only did we want to see the splendors of Patagonia with its eerie mountain ranges at the end of the world but we also wanted to visit Easter Island. The nearest jumping-off spot for all of that was Chile.

At this point, let's pause to consider the geography of the southern tip of South America. The first thing to remember is that Chile is a long, narrow coastal country flanked by the Pacific on its western side and the Andes Mountain on the eastern side. More precisely it is 2,700 miles long but only 110 miles wide on average. Neighboring Argentina also narrows at its most southern projection so much so that it is hard to tell which country is which.

Southern Chile

After a few days of consideration about this venture, we decided: Yes. Let's go for it. I was always intrigued about the bottom of the world in the Southern Hemisphere. We had already seen it from the southern tip of the South Island in New Zealand. A view here would be even more southern and we would get to gaze on the Straits of Magellan and maybe points farther south. Then there was the lure of far off and remote Easter Island with its mysterious statues known as the Moai.

So I booked the flights for Chile. Target date: mid-December 2015 to mid-January 2016. Once the flights were secured, I then plotted out our itinerary: First to the capital city of Chile, Santiago, for a few days and then a meet up with Vanessa who would be done with her weeklong Patagonia hiking trek. Next, all of us would fly to Easter Island for six nights. After that back to Santiago and a goodbye to Vanessa who would return to the states. My wife Yvonne and I would then fly south to Chile's Lake District for a couple of days and then on to Patagonia where we would rent a car and root around in the mountains at the end of the world. There. Confusing isn't it? But as the reader will see, it became a lot more complicated and confusing thanks to the Chilean airline LAN going on strike.

Nonetheless, here is how it went:

1. DEPARTURE

Sunday, Dec. 12, 2015

The departure drill. Driving from Pueblo to Denver International Airport a 109 miles north is a major project. About a two hour drive on I-25. Since we had to be at the airport at 9:30 a.m. for our 11:30 a.m. flight to Dallas, we decided to skip the hassle of an early morning drive through the commuter traffic around Colorado Springs and check into a motel near the airport the night before. This is a common practice in Colorado for people coming from the furthest reaches of the state who have to make a morning flight. In fact, there one main road, Tower Road, chock full of motels that cater to this group of travelers. But making this trek a day early was enough to make us yearn for our 15-minute commute by cab to O'Hare Airport, a mere ten miles away from our former house in North Edgebrook, Chicago.

Nonetheless, all was well as we bedded down and went to sleep in the Quality Inn on Tower Road. Then the telephone rang. The voice claimed that it was the Front Desk and that they misplaced my credit card info when I checked in. Could I please give it to them over the phone?

Half asleep, I dug out my American Express credit card and at the voice's instruction, read off my name. But when the voice asked for my credit card number, a little bell went off in my head. I had seen the clerk running my card through their card machine when I checked in. How could they lose that digital info? Something was goofy here, I thought. So I told the voice to hold on, that I would get up and come down to the desk to straighten this out.

The voice then said, "That won't be necessary. You can do it in the morning and hung up." So I went back to sleep.

Monday, Dec. 13

The next morning before breakfast, I went down to the Front Desk and asked the receptionist on duty about the midnight call about my losing my credit card info. The receptionist pulled up my check-in info on the computer and said "We have all your information, Mr. Brown. You must have gotten a scam call. That happens now and then. Good thing you didn't give your card number."

"No kidding," I responded.

She further explained to me that these scam artists go around phoning motel rooms at random at various motels and ask for credit card info claiming they were from the front desk and somehow they had lost it.

Hmm, I thought. The scams are already happening and we are not even in Chile yet.

***

Once breakfasted and our car parked in the Canopy Parking lot nearby, we took a shuttle over to the main terminal of the DIA airport. Even at 9:30 a.m., the place was a madhouse. I guess it was the early Christmas rush. It took forty-five minutes to pass through security. We arrived at our flight gate around about 10:30 an hour early which made me wonder why the airlines insist you arrive two hours early for a domestic flight.

The flight to Dallas on American Airlines was mercifully short sitting as we were in cramped economy seats in the back for about two hours. We got to know the Dallas Fort Worth airport rather well since we had a six-hour layover for our flight to Santiago, Chile. We could have taken a later afternoon flight from Denver but that would have given us only a half-hour to make the connecting flight. And since that was in an entirely different terminal unfamiliar to us, I booked the early flight.

So how did we pass the time in DFW? We made our way over to the International Terminal gate and basically chilled. We read mostly, wandered around and ate. We even took a little doze in some chairs in a quiet area of the terminal.

Finally, it was time to board our American Airlines flight around 9:15 p.m. which would take about ten hours. Ten hours! I thought. That's like flying to Europe. South America, it seemed to me, was a lot closer. Actually, that's not the case. Dallas to Chile is only a couple of hundred miles closer than from Dallas to Paris. (i.e. 4,948 airline miles).

Whatever, we did have exit aisles seats on this international flight with lots of legroom so we were comfortable throughout the flight. Of course, I had to pay a few hundred bucks extra for those seats but it was well worth it. We read, watched movies, slept, drank and dined on pretty good food with a slight South American touch. Unlike many domestic flights, the flight attendants were sharp, efficient, bilingual and quite attractive.

2. SANTIAGO

Tuesday, Dec. 15

We finally arrived at Santiago Airport around 9:30 a.m. local time. The airport was a zoo, crowded and chaotic beyond belief. Only a couple of passport control agents were on duty in their booths although two other booths were empty thus creating long lines. It took almost an hour to go through customs and passport control.

We were tired and grumpy after the long flight and still had to manhandle our carry-on luggage. I had on my backpack but I was also carrying Yvonne's shoulder bag all loaded up. She was dealing with another bag also loaded to the gills with god knows what. We had had several arguments about these two bags. I maintained that one bag for her was good enough but to no avail. After all, we had two large suitcases that we would retrieve once through customs. How much luggage do you really need for a three-and-half week trip?

When we finally got to a manned booth, the passport control agent in the booth grunted a "Buenos Dias," flipped through our passports, stamped them and then issued us a 90-day tourist visa.

Moving on to the baggage carrousel, we retrieved our luggage and rolled it over to the baggage customs agent who merely waved us through. Already checked and x-rayed, I assumed.

Next were out into the main terminal which was also a madhouse. We made our way to a taxi counter and plunked out about 15,000 pesos in Chilean currency for a ride into the city. That was about 20 bucks. (765 CLP = 1.00 USD)

Then we stepped outside and a cabbie dispatcher pointed to a nice new, shiny cab for us, a Toyota, I think. The driver gave us a nod and a big smile as he hopped out and stowed our suitcases in his trunk. We piled in and were soon off wending our way through a labyrinth of airport roads until we came to an expressway and discovered how far out of town the airport was from downtown Santiago, some 32 kilometers

As we cruised along we could see a range of brown mountains looming off in the distance. Of course, these were the Andes. The driver who spoke some English observed that it was a remarkably clear day for Santiago which is sometimes engulfed in "brumosa." Of course, what he meant was Santiago was often smoggy especially in summer when the emissions from cars and wood-burning fumes are backed up to the mountains. Actually, Santiago is one of the smoggiest cities in South America

As we got closer to Santiago, the outskirts started building up until we could see from a point on the elevated expressway a vast sprawling megalopolis that seemed to go on forever, similar to Los Angeles. Santiago is, of course, the largest city in Chile with a population of some seven million.

Anyway, it was smooth sailing for us on our expressway until we took a cutoff to a crosstown expressway into the inner city. Here, the traffic increased but for us the urban scenery was interesting for this section of Santiago was filled with gleaming skyscrapers in the latest modern design, some of them similar to the modern skyscrapers in Chicago.

Santiago, Chile

Once past this modern section we turned off the expressway, and into the interior streets, past parklands, mansions and a stately looking museum. Minutes later, we entered the Bella Arts District. Here the narrow streets were lined with art galleries, bars, restaurants and outdoor cafes. Many of the buildings were covered with murals, very colorful artistic murals. This was not your average street art.

Bella Arts District

Street Murals

Soon we arrived at our hotel which was not a hotel but rather a hostel called the Andes Hostel on Monjitas Street. This hostel featured dormitory-type lodging for the budget traveler, mostly young travelers but it also had regular rooms with bathrooms. That's what we had reserved while trying to be cheap. Downtown hotels in Santiago were expensive and I decided if we were going to blow money on this trip it would be in Patagonia and Easter Island, not Santiago.

We thought the Andes Hostel was a trip. It had a great bar and lounge decorated in 1960s hippy chic. They even had live nightly music of some sort and a complimentary breakfast. Our room while not luxurious was clean and comfortable. The bathroom, however, was a little cranky. Not much hot water, low water pressure, etc. But overall, it was quite doable for the four nights we were staying here and the 20-somethings staying here were a delight and brought back memories of our youth hostel days in Europe in the 1960s. Oh, a few other geezer types were staying here as well so we felt very welcome.

But no sooner had we got settled in and were about to go out to explore the neighborhood when a breathless, heavyset lady with a British accent came bursting through the door exclaiming:

"The little rot-gut bastards made off with my daypack! Quick, quick, call the cops," she ordered the clerk on the reception desk.

The clerk tried to get more information about what the daypack looked like.

"It's a bleeding tan daypack like hundreds of others around here. And it's got my passport and a lot of money inside. I'm fucked if I can't get it back," she barked.

The clerk nodded and dialed the police. The lady was hovering over him breathing heavily as if she had been running a marathon.

She then turned to several of us gathered around in the lobby and explained how it happened:

"Be Careful, people. Here I was, just walking along enjoying the sights around here, right close to this hotel, when unknown to me somebody squirted some white stuff all over my back and my daypack. Maybe it was a kid on a bike that had just zoomed past."

"Then a teenage girl came up with a handkerchief and pointed to my day pack saying in broken English that I had bird poop on my back and daypack. She offered to clean it off and while doing so offered to hold my daypack."

"So I took off my daypack, saw that what looked like bird shit on it and then stupidly gave her the daypack to hold. Then in a split second, she was gone, fast as a fox. I tried to run after her but being a bit hefty and not in good health, I gave up after a half block and returned to the hotel."

By this time, a cop had shown up, looking very concerned and started taking notes. He spoke some English and explained they would do their best to retrieve the daypack but warned that it might not be possible.

At this point, we had heard enough and left the hotel to start walking around the neighborhood but we were carrying no day pack. Our money and passports were safely tucked away in our money belts strapped around our waist. "Let the little fuckers try to get that" I mused.

We didn't get very far in our walk, just a couple of blocks until we came out to a large park, Parque Forestal. It was now very hot and humid so we sat in the shade on a bench for a while and then repaired to a nearby café/restaurant for a late lunch that was also to serve as dinner. We had a tasty chunk of barbeque pork rib with sides and two Crystal beers. With full stomachs and the buzz of the beers in the heat, the day was over for us. We returned to the hostel and crashed for a siesta.

Around six, we roused ourselves and decided to venture out again to see what we could see. Of course, with these long summer days down here in the southern hemisphere, the sun was still high in the sky shining brightly but a cool breeze was blowing.

I could imagine the scene back in Chicago, our former home, with snow piling up and Arctic blasts of wind coming down from Canada. This was much nicer. In addition, we saw few signs of the approaching Christmas holidays. Nary a wreath nor a decorated Christmas tree. What a relief!

Dutifully following Yvonne from one shop to another, we perused the offerings. Many featured local art. Yvonne who was an art junky was impressed with some of the items. She even knew about the major painters in Chile, "This stuff is quite good, original with a hint of the surreal. Many in the vein of Mario Gomez," she said pointing to a poster reproduction of a Gomez painting.

Mario Gomez Painting

"Mario who?"

"Mario Gomez."

"How do you know about him?"

"Oh, I did a little art research before coming down here. He's one of the greats of Chilean art. And often compared to Salvador Dali."

"Oh."

End of discussion.

After strolling around for a while, we returned to the hotel and had a beer in the lounge bar, which was now filled with the 20-somethings talking about their day's adventures.

Feeling somewhat out of place, we took a table in the corner and watched the youth scene from afar. Young, carefree and adventurous. Backpacks strewn all over the floor. The scene made us wish for a return to yesterday but alas, it was too late for that. Eventually, we took our leave and made our way up to our room, closing the curtains since it was still daylight outside. End of day one in Chile.

Wednesday, Dec. 16

The next morning after a fairly decent breakfast buffet, we left around ten to visit the nearby National Museum on the edge of the Parque Forestal. This stately museum of fine arts is known more precisely as the Museo Nacional de Bellas Artes. It's the premier museum in all of Chile and features the most important works by Chilean and South American artists. This museum was free and we spent almost two hours in it wandering around.

Museo Nacional de Bellas Artes

The main entrance hall featured rows of sculptures in marble and bronze, all recreated samples of ancient Roman and Greek sculptures. The south wing had displays of traditional European art with paintings by Italian, Spanish and Flemish painters.

However, it was in the north wing that we saw what we had come to see—a vast collection of Chilean and South American art featuring artists like Luis Vargas Rosas and Roberto Matta.

Roberto Matta

Also as a special treat, we saw an exhibition of Orozco, the Mexican painter and also an early Diego Riviera in his cubist phase.

Diego Rivera

As interesting as the paintings were, the interior architecture of the museum was as inspiring as well. It featured a glass-encased atrium which bathed the artwork below in natural light.

Glass Atrium

Once done with the National Museum, we walked over to a food truck and bought a couple of chacareros. Chacareros are a Chilean tortilla sandwich filled with pork, tomatoes, beans and chili peppers. Quite tasty. After scarfing these down while sitting on park bench, we then hiked over several blocks to the center of old Santiago, namely the Plaza de Armas.

While walking over there on a crowded sidewalk, a slick-looking dude walked past us brushing by my daypack which I carried slung over one shoulder. Then he paused before a newsstand as we continued walking on. Next thing I knew he brushed by me again. I gave him a look like "Get the fuck away from me." Then he practically ran off.

Luckily, I had nothing much in my daypack except a guidebook and a cheapie little camera. My wallet with my dough and passport was all in my money belt. Yvonne who was walking by my side noticed this too and said that from now on she would walk a couple of paces behind me to keep an eye out for this sort of thing.

Soon we came out to the Plaza de Armas, a wide, pleasant plaza dotted with towering palm trees, a garden in the center and a lot a people lounging about on benches.

Plaza de Armas

We also saw a couple of mounted policemen entertaining a group of kids. At one point one of the cops picked up a small child and plunked him down in front of him on his horse. No doubt a thrill for the lad.

Horse Friendly

Following that, we turned our attention to the cathedral dominating the square, the Santiago Metropolitan Cathedral. We entered its portals and were immediately struck by its highly decorated Baroque interior.

Santiago Metropolitan Cathedral

This cathedral was the descendent of the first cathedral in the city founded by the Spanish Conquistador, Pedro de Valdiva in 1541. Today, it is the home base for the Archdiocese of Chile.

Pedro de Valdiva

A large statue of Valdiva mounted on a horse stood right outside the cathedral making it a perfect spot for kids to play on.

The other major attraction on the Plaza de Armas was the Museo Historico Nacional which was closed for renovation. No matter. We had had enough museum-going for the day.

One thing we missed seeing was the La Moneda Palace, the presidential palace only blocks away on Plaza de la Constitution.

La Moneda Palace

This where President Salvador Allende ruled from 1970 to 1973 until he was deposed in a hail of gunfire by the Chilean Army under the command of August Pinochet who also had the palace bombed for good measure. Supposedly, you can still see the bullet holes in the courtyard. But we missed all that. No matter, we would see and hear a lot about Allende before we were through with Santiago.

Done with our quick look around, we headed off to one of the banks lining the square where I changed a few hundred dollars into Chilean pesos. For some reason, my Chilean pesos were going fast. I mean when one Chilean peso is worth only .0013 of a U.S. dollar, you have to lug around a lot of pesos even in the higher dominations.

With that little chore done, we walked back to our hotel loaded with pesos in my daypack. Yvonne walked behind me as a rearguard watching for pickpockets. I felt like I was in a Brinks armored guard procession.

That was about it for the day. We returned to our hotel and had a beer in the lounge while we once again grooved on the lost youth scene. After a while we repaired to a café/restaurant next door and had a rather mediocre meal of overcooked lamb and soggy French fries. Washed down with yet another beer. After that, we went up to our room and watched some Spanish language television that we could barely make out.

3. MEMORY MUSEUM

Thursday, Dec. 17

We started the day with a hike up the highest hill in Santiago which happened to be only a few blocks from our hotel. It was called the Cerro San Cristobal and it featured a 22-foot state of the Virgin Mary. She sat on top of a sanctuary dedicated to the Immaculate Conception.

Cerro San Cristobal

It was an easy hike along a road and a path that wound its way up the hill. Once on top, we were treated with views of the city but from this angle, it was a city laden with high rises, many of them cheap looking. Looking in the other direction, we could see that the hill capped an extensive park system that sprawled along for miles.

Santiago, Chile

Off in the distance, hazy in the smog, we could make out the Andes Mountains which came right down to the city limits. After hanging around for a while on the hill, we hiked back down and noticed an abandoned cable car system just sitting there somewhat intact. Word was it was put out of service due to an exploding gearbox a few years ago but that there were plans to put it back in service someday soon.

Back at our hostel for a quick sandwich lunch which Yvonne had prepared, we set off again. This time our destination was the Museum of Memory and Human Rights, a museum dedicated to the illegal overthrow of Salvador Allende and the subsequent years. Since it was quite far away we decided to take the Santiago subway which turned out to be very clean and modern. I thought back to the grubby subways of Chicago and New York.

Santiago Subway

By riding the subway we got there in a matter of minutes with a stop right outside the museum. And at first, glance, what a nice, sleek looking museum it was.

Memory Museum

We entered the museum and encountered two lovely ladies at the admission desk. We paid our entrance fee and then one of them offered us an audio tour recorder in English for another small fee. We were tempted but based on past experience we found such audio devices quite annoying. Essentially, you have to listen to some boring narrator drone on and on about a particular exhibit ad infinitum. We were confident that based on our general knowledge of those years of the overthrow of Allende and the Pinochet regime, we could make out the exhibits. So we politely refused. We then asked if some of the exhibits had explanations in English. The lady replied that indeed they did.

First a bit of background on this museum. It was relatively new with construction completed in 2010. The museum, officially known as the "The Museum of Memory and Human Rights" was dedicated to commemorate the victims of human rights violations during the civic-military regime led by Augusto Pinochet between 1973 and 1990. And what a bloody regime it was with thousands of political prisoners many of whom were simply "disappeared" and were never seen again.

As we wandered through we saw that the first room was dedicated to the universal challenge of human rights with generic displays of people suffering under other autocratic regimes.

The second room focused on Pinochet's military coup of September 11, 1973. As mentioned before, Pinochet, backed by the CIA overthrew the constitutionally elected Salvador Allende whose only sin was that he was a socialist. This hall had the photos and the film clips of Pinochet's soldiers attacking the presidential palace, of course ending with a photo of the dead Allende.

Dead Salvador Allende

Rooms 3 through 6, displayed film, photos and various documents describing the repression and the techniques of torture such as electric shock and surgical disfigurement, namely the gouging and removal of eyeballs. Everywhere were wall displays of photographs of "the disappeared."

The Disappeared

Only a fraction of the "disappeared" remains have been recovered in various burial sites. Hundreds more were reportedly tossed from government helicopters hovering over the vast Pacific.

Rooms 7 through 11, described the waning days of the Pinochet regime, his unexpected loss in a referendum in 1988 and the return to a more or less democratic government in the late 80s and early 90s.

There was supposedly a reconciliation process under the new democratic government of Patricio Aylwin. But this process turned out to be a sham and let many Pinochet supporters and enablers off the hook. Even today, many former Pinochet henchmen are living a rich lifestyle in hillside mansions above Santiago.

This ominous detail was mentioned to us by one of the ladies at the admission desk after we were done going through the museum. It came about because we had paused at the desk to mention how great this museum was in depicting this dark period in Chile.

Speaking in excellent English, she replied, "Yes, I know because I was a little girl living through it and my father was a victim of the Pinochet regime. To this day we still don't know what happened to him. Poor papa is probably in a mass grave somewhere or more likely he was tossed into the ocean."

She stated this matter of factly and finished looking off through the large entrance hall windows in the direction of the Pacific.

Following this head-spinning tour of the Memory Museum, we returned to our hostel and relaxed until it was dinner time. Then we headed out again to a nearby neighborhood in the Bella Vista district known for its many fashionable restaurants and counter-culture atmosphere, something like Haight Ashbury back in the day. We settled on one highly recommended place called "Les Assassins," evidently named after a Paris restaurant and night club.

Self-Explanatory

Although the restaurant was inspired by French cuisine, we settled on a grilled sea bass dish common to Chile situated as it was on the shores of the Pacific. That with a bottle of the local Chilean chardonnay completed our meal.

4. HILTON PURGATORY

Friday, Dec. 18

This was the day we said goodbye to Santiago. We were going to meet up with Vanessa who was flying in from Patagonia in the late afternoon, then spend a night at a hotel near the airport. The next day we were scheduled to fly out to Easter Island. However, first thing we wanted to do before checking out of the hostel was find the house of Neruda, the famous Chilean poet. His house called La Chascona was nearby and supposedly something to see.

So here we were walking along Bella Vista Boulevard when a guy on a bike whizzed by and splashed my backpack with a white liquid that looked like bird shit. I didn't even feel it and was clueless that it had happened for a few seconds until a little Indian girl with a Kleenex came rushing up to me and offered to wipe it off my backpack with a Kleenex. Wise to this trick by now, Yvonne just behind me grabbed the Kleenex from the girl and told her to scram which she did, hustling off quickly and disappearing into the crowd.

Meanwhile, another English lady who was walking behind us saw the whole thing, told us it was the standard bird shit trick.

"You are lucky, hon. If you had that taken that backpack off, the little buggers would have made off of that."

"Yeah, we have run into this before," I replied. "Another lady lost her day pack right outside of where we were staying, passport and all. Makes you wonder why bother coming to Santiago."

"Bloody right. The place has some issues. But I live here and work at the British Embassy right up the road so I have to put up with it."

Trudging on, we headed over to the Cerro San Cristobol hill at the foot of which was the Nureda house, La Chascona near the defunct tramway. We managed to spot it tucked up against the hillside even though it was nearly covered by foliage from trees and underbrush. The home was supposedly built to resemble a ship but it didn't look like it to us. It was just a house up against a hill with a balcony railing.

La Chascona

We knew there were tours of the place but we figured we didn't have time for that. By this point, we were tired and hot and wanted nothing more to do than to hit an outdoor café, have an early lunch. Then pack up and head to the airport where we would check into the Hilton Garden Inn.

Hilton Garden Hotel

Around two, after another long cab ride to the airport, we arrived at the Hilton and then an hour later we met Vanessa who had just arrived in the domestic terminal. After all the hugs and kisses upon her arrival, we looked her over. She was still dusty and dirty from her weeklong hike through the mountains of Patagonia but she was full of adventure stories about her trek.

"Those mountains in Torres del Paine are unreal. Like something you might see on the moon. Strait up, jagged, no erosion or anything. We had a great time hiking through them."

"Did you climb one of them?" I asked.

"No dad, we just hiked around their bases. We got up pretty high though. The biggest hassle was the rain. It rained just about every day. I was glad I had my poncho."

She then showed us a photo like this that she took with her cell phone.

Torres del Paine

I replied, "Impressive. Surreal but right now let's catch a cab and get over to our hotel. You can fill us in later."

Back at the hotel, I went on-line to find out about the status of our flight to Easter Island scheduled for tomorrow. Was it on or was it off? Alas, it was off. According to the LAN website, it had just been canceled even though strike negotiations were underway. I had thought that surely after a few days, such a strike by LAN, the only major airline in Chile, would be resolved.

However, the lady at the tour desk told us that the latest rumors were that the strike could end at any minute and that flights would resume. She urged us to be ready to go at a moment's notice tomorrow.

Confident that we would soon be getting out of here, we relaxed in our four-star hotel. Swam in the rooftop pool, baked in the summer heat and had a great dinner.

Thus ended our first day in what we would soon come to call "Hilton purgatory."

Saturday, Dec. 19

The next morning, after a delicious breakfast buffet, I tried again to confirm reservations for Easter Island. This time I managed to get through to a LAN representative on the telephone. She told me in English that flights to Easter Island through the 22nd of December had been canceled. Negotiations had apparently broken down with no end in sight.

Shit! Now what? Were we ever going to get out of here? Let alone to Easter Island. Meanwhile, Vanessa was getting antsy. She had allotted seven days for Easter Island and those days were slipping away. Her return flight to the U.S. was on December 27th, thankfully on Delta Airlines not on LAN. She suggested that we forget about Easter Island for the time being and instead rent a car to explore the north coast of Chile for the next five days or so.

"So you want to give up on Easter Island?" I asked.

"Yes, Dad, it doesn't look like it's in the cards for me. Someday I will see it. Probably in conjunction with a ski trip I would like to take down here. Anyway, I've heard that the north coast of Chile is interesting too. There's even an excursion that we can take into the foothills of the Andes in Chile's wine growing country," she continued.

"Yes, we have heard about that too," I mused. "So why not. It sounds better than sitting around here in this hotel waiting for a flight to Easter Island."

Being retired, Yvonne and I were very flexible. We had no great deadline for our return to the States. Add to that, I had been told by the LAN representative that LAN had waived all the penalties for flight changes while the strike was going on.

So I sat down in our rather spacious room at a nice large desk and opened my little Samsung tablet computer and proceeded to figure all this out.

First, we planned out our excursion up the north coast with Vanessa returning by the 26th so Vanessa could fly off a day later.

Once Vanessa was off for the states, Yvonne and I would then resume our original itinerary and fly down the Patagonia where we had hotel reservations at various places. The only catch was I had to cancel a couple of nights in the Lake District and fly directly to Punta Arenas on the Magellan Strait and the jumping-off spot to Chile's Patagonia.

I spent the entire day, re-arranging our itinerary, reserving a car for our jog up north and making hotel reservations in Vina Del Mar and La Serena, a couple of north coast cities.

And last but not least, hoping against hope that the LAN strike would be over by January 6th when we would be back from our sojourn in Patagonia, I tried to make reservations for Easter Island on January 7. But still no luck. I concluded if the strike was not resolved by then, we would say so much for Easter Island and Yvonne and I would fly home.

Sunday, Dec. 20

The next morning I attempted to pick up our rental car at the airport but there was a long line at the Avis counter and a lot of pissed off people. It seemed somebody or some computer had screwed up the reservation system and as a result, few cars were on hand to rent.

After spending an hour standing in the line, I finally got to the counter where the agent told me that my car would not be available for at least a couple of hours. Rather than go back to the hotel, I hung around the terminal for those hours, having first another morning coffee and then later when I was hungry, a McDonald's burger with a beer.

Finally, around one, my car was available but by that time I was resigned to spending another day in Hilton purgatory. I procured my car and drove out of the terminal following a labyrinth of streets until after a few false turns, I stumbled upon my hotel. We spent the rest of the day lounging around the pool and having a couple of Pisco Sours, the national drink, a grape brandy that packs a punch. Later we had another fine meal with the ever-present Chilean bass.

5. NORTH SHORE

Monday, Dec. 21

Early the next morning, we were off on our jaunt up Chile's north coast. Now, we were not going all the way up. After all, from the airport to the northern border with Peru it was about two thousand kilometers (1,200 miles) much of it through sparsely populated desert country. Nor were we going to dip inland into the Atacama Desert known for its high altitudes and brilliant star gazing.

No, we were going a mere 478 kilometers no further than the popular beach resort town of La Serena. And even then, we would be traveling along leisurely, stopping off at several places including Valparaiso and Vina del Mar.

First up, however, was Lago Penuelas, a small provincial park located in the rolling hills just off the main highway to Valparaiso. We didn't spend much time here but the setting was peaceful and relaxing with the water gently lapping on the shores of this reservoir lake.

Moving on, we came to the outskirts of Valparaiso, the third largest city in Chile and once the most important Pacific port in Chile before the Panama Canal was built. You see, all those clipper ships in the 19th century had to have somewhere to repair and re-supply after rounding the storm-ravaged Cape Horn at the tip of South America.

Once in town and going along the main drag, we could see that Valparaiso still functioned as a major port what with its docks, cranes, containers and tramp steamers. But outside of the business district, the town itself struck me as a dump with row after row of decaying houses up and down its hillsides. The only bright spot was the blindingly brilliant graffiti that covered many of these homes and buildings.

Valparaiso

Yvonne was intrigued by all of this and wanted to stop but Vanessa and I wanted to move on to the nearby town of Vina del Mar where we planned to spend a couple of days. I promised Yvonne that she would have her chance to come back and groove on the artistic splendors of Valparaiso.

Fourteen kilometers later along the coastal road, we came to the outskirts of Vina de Mar. Once in town, it struck us as an upscale resort. Something like a mini-Cannes. Driving along we passed by a massive seaside casino, a vision straight out of Monaco and maybe a James Bond movie.

We checked into the local Best Western a few blocks away from the ocean but reasonably priced and then walked around town for a while before returning to our hotel, having dinner and then crashing. Something about the sea air, I guess.

Tuesday, Dec. 22

Vanessa and I spent the day wandering around Vina del Mar, checking out the casino and a local museum that focused on Easter Island.

Yvonne was off with a group on a special tour of Valparaiso. A wild-looking dude had come into the hotel last night while we were eating dinner touting a special art tour of Valparaiso. He said he had two other couples from the hotel who were going and he was looking for a third. Vanessa and I demurred but Yvonne was eager to go, so she signed up with these words:

"Allan and Vanessa, you don't know what you are missing. This should be quite interesting. That graffiti is world-renowned."

"Duly noted," I replied. "Tell us all about it when you return."

Later when we ventured out, one of our first stops was the Fonck Museum. Surprisingly here was an extensive collection of Easter Island artifacts including a giant moai, which was stationed out front.

Fonck Museum

The lady tour guide was great as she led us through room after room of artifacts and outlined the tragic history of Easter Island. She told us that all of this had been gathered by an Austrian Archeologist, a Mr. Fritz Felbermayer, during the thirties and amassed what was considered the best collection of Easter Island artifacts outside of the island itself.

By the time we got through this enlightening tour, I was more eager than ever to go there despite all the hassle and expense. Of course, this tour was also a godsend for Vanessa who was going to miss Easter Island. At least now she got a glimpse of its ancient culture in this little museum.

Following the museum, we drove over to the James Bond casino, known simply as the Casino of Vina del Mar. This was a huge white elephant looking building, somewhat in the art deco style.

Casino de Vina del Mar

Inside, it was cavernous but elegant with never-ending gaming halls yet nearly deserted. Maybe it was too early for the high rollers. Of course, there were rows and rows of electronic slot machines in other chambers and other assorted video games, all the bane, I think today's casinos. Still, it was easy to imagine James Bond sophisticates passing an evening here playing baccarat. We did notice that the whole oceanside of the casino had been built out to form a luxury hotel, thus destroying its architectural unity.

Getting near lunchtime, we hiked over to the city beach a few yards from the casino and planted ourselves in a beachside eatery with a great view of the rolling Pacific. I say rolling because the Pacific was rough today thanks to a cool wind blowing in from offshore. But that didn't stop the many kids from wading out into the surf with their boogie boards and little surfboards to try to ride the waves. All of this would have been great if it had been warmer.

Here we were in the Southern Hemisphere in the middle of their summer with temperatures only in the low 70s. The water temperature was even worse, down in the 60s thanks to the Humboldt Current which ran north along the coast of Chile. So these little guys were freezing their butts off, even though a few that had on wet suit tops on. But for us, nice and warm behind a windbreak glass, with a Chilean tortilla sandwich and a tasty beer, all was well in Vina del Mar.

Following an hour of lounging around the beachfront, we returned to our car in the casino parking lot and drove around town and through some of the outskirts. All in all, very peaceful. A perfect little retirement community for the Chileans. Something similar to the beach communities north of San Diego. Around three we went back to our hotel and for a little siesta.

Of course, when Yvonne returned later that afternoon, she raved about her graffiti tour of Valparaiso. "You and Vanessa really missed it."

"No doubt but you missed a great museum about Easter Island," I replied.

"Ha, I'll see plenty of that when we actually get there. Right now, I'll take Valparaiso."

"Well, Vanessa and I had a very relaxing day on the beachfront. We also checked out that big casino. Then we came back here and rested. So now we will be raring to go tomorrow."

Wednesday, Dec. 23

The next morning we took off early for a long drive to La Serena up the coast about 444 kilometers (275 miles). Most of this drive on the Pan American highway was along the oceanfront through desert-like terrain. As noted before, here it was the middle of summer but all these long, powder white beaches with a rolling blue surf were deserted. Nobody was about except for a camper van parked here and there and a couple of fishermen surfcasting. A scene like this would be unthinkable in similar stretches in Southern California.

About the only bright spot other than the scenery we were passing through was that we could make some real time here pushing it way over the speed limit to about 128 km/h (80 mph) on this nicely paved road. This despite Yvonne's constant nagging. As a result, we were on the outskirts of La Serena by about two p.m.

Since we arrived early here, we decided to kill some time driving around town. The first thing we discovered was that La Serena is really two towns—the new town with all the resort hotels on the beach and the older still intact colonial town inland.

Driving through the new town, we could see not much of interest here just a wall of high rise hotels, condos, tourist shops and barely populated wide beaches. I guess the water was still cold here.

La Serena Beach

Turning into the old town, we were struck by its colonial charm with a large church dominating the central square and a lot of well-preserved 18th and 19th century structures. It was here in this section that we had booked two rooms at a cheap hostel type hotel. I think it was called Hostel Solaris. Vanessa declared the place a "dumpola" but it was not bad. It was clean and comfortable and breakfast was included. By now, Yvonne and I were tired of the so-called luxury hotels like the Hilton Gardens. We wanted to be in the middle of the old city action and soak up the colonial atmosphere.

La Serena

After getting settled we did just that by wandering around the main plaza which was overflowing with temporary Christmas markets and hordes of last-minute Christmas shoppers. Or were they really last minute? It seemed to me that Chileans didn't sweat Christmas very much until a couple of days before and then all the decorations and Xmas hullabaloo came on full steam. Actually, it was refreshing and of course, you have to remember that Christmas down here was in the middle of summer so it was shorts and tee shirts and halter tops everywhere. It reminded me of Hawaii at Christmas.

We viewed a lot of this from a restaurant balcony that overlooked the plaza. This joint had been recommended by my guidebook and while the margaritas were great and abundant, and the view of the plaza below spectacular, our main fish dish was mediocre, some sort of fish jambalaya in a sauce over rice. As a result, we barely touched it and ordered a big plate of fries instead. Not to be deterred, we ordered another round of drinks and hung out here until twilight when all the Christmas lights came on, with a lot of tinny Xmas music.

After that, we retired to our quarters and got ready for a big day on the morrow.

Thursday, Dec. 24

This morning we drove up the Elqui Valley about 100 K east of La Serena. This was a major wine growing region in Chile similar to Napa Valley. It was fertile valley set between the dry foothills of the Andes, a valley known mainly for vines producing the famous Chilean drink, the Pisco Sour.

Elqui Valley

As we drove along, we passed vineyard after vineyard until we came to the main town in these parts, Vicuna. This was a small colonial type berg also very busy with Christmas activities. While we were parked on the square, a pickup truck rolled by with a red-suited Santa throwing out little gifts and candy to a bunch of kids. We then decided on a mid-morning snack ourselves so we had coffee and slices of delicious homemade lemon pie at a local café full of coffee table books about the splendors of the region.

Vicuna

Following that Vanessa and I walked around the square with Yvonne a few paces behind us. She said she was watching some guy who had made a couple of passes by Vanessa and me, acting suspicious and eyeing my small backpack. On his third pass, Yvonne yelled at him and told him to bug off in English. He got the message and disappeared.

After passing an hour or so in Vicuna we continued up the road into an ever-narrowing valley with the dirt foothills of the Andes looming larger and larger. At some points, we could see the peaks of the full-scale Andes themselves. Now here is where it got dicey. The nicely paved road turned rough as we passed through several small, tumbled down settlements on the roadside.

At one in particular, we felt we had entered some latter-day hippy commune. Indeed, through our open windows, we could smell the incense and the pot. Here and there young guys and gals in long Indian type gowns wandered about. One couple turned and waved at us.

We were tempted to stop but Vanessa thought the whole place was weird urged us to turn around. Our hippy days long past, I did turn around and headed back towards Vicuna or rather to another sight that we had skipped coming up the road, the Observatorio Cancana.

It is claimed that besides having a perfect climate, this region boasts the clearest skies in the world and thus, is a perfect spot to gaze upon the heavens at night. And while the skies were indeed a crystalline blue, there was no chance of us hanging around until dark to view the stars. Nonetheless, we did stop and check out the observatory. Usually, there are tours of the place but a guard informed us that all was closed on Christmas Eve. Still even looking at the observatory from a distance, it was quite impressive.

Observatorio Cancana

From this spot, we had an even better view of the Andes range and I had to admit that while impressive with their soaring heights, these were still ugly, stark brown mountains devoid of vegetation or even snow at their summits. I thought they contrasted poorly to my beautiful Rockies and well-forested California Sierras.

Following this day-long jaunt up the Elqui Valley, we returned to La Serena, explored the town a bit more and found a much better hole-in-the-wall restaurant on a side street. We had a killer fish dish and a round of Pisco Sours.

And that was the end of our exploration of northern Chile although we realized that we had missed much, mainly the Atacama Desert and Chile's newest region that it had annexed from Peru known as the Arica y Parinacota Region along its northern border.

Tomorrow we return to our Hilton Garden purgatory where we would try to figure out what to do next. Hey, this is Christmas Eve! Maybe Santa would have some ideas.

Friday, Dec. 25

The next morning the old section of La Serena was ghost- town quite even though it was Christmas day. I guess all the big celebrations had gone on Christmas Eve. No matter, it was peaceful for us—no screaming kids, no opening of presents. No, all we had to do was load up our rental car and get out of town. Once on the outskirts of La Serena, the Pan American highway was deserted. It was like an end of the world scene but it did allow me to haul ass back to Santiago. Despite Yvonne's protest, I averaged over 130 km an hour (80mph) with no sign of cops and before we knew it, three hours later we were back at our hotel, the Hilton Gardens near the airport.

By now, the staff knew who we were. I joked that our stay here was like a homecoming. The cute clerk at the reception desk nodded in agreement. The only problem was we still were not certain how long that would be. But we decided to forget all of that and spent the rest of the day by the pool. We then had an extra special multi-course Christmas dinner with sea bass and a tasty fowl of some sort and an excellent bottle of wine followed by a round of Pisco Sours, now and then gazing at a lone Christmas tree sparkling in the lobby. Where was Santa now?

6. PUNTA ARENAS

Saturday, Dec. 26

The first thing in the morning I dumped the rental car at the airport and then we spent the rest of the day at the hotel. But hey guess what? The LAN strike was over and I was finally able to book a flight to Easter Island from Jan 7 to 13. I also booked a four-star resort hotel on the island as well. I don't believe it.

In the meantime, we would be flying down to Punta Arenas and Patagonia as initially scheduled except we had to forego the whole Lake District portion of the trip in central Chile.

This was too bad because I had been looking forward to a couple of tranquil days at a lakeside hotel surrounded by mountains and several inactive volcanos. It seemed like a good place to relax and engage in various activities such as swimming and boating as well as hiking around viewing these inactive volcanos.

But what intrigued me the most was the German influence in the Lake District that featured many Germanic settlements with Bavarian architecture and whatnot. Although German immigration to Chile in this area began in the 19th century, the Lake District was also notable for harboring high-level Nazi refugees, somewhat similar to what happened in neighboring Argentina. But that's a whole other story.

No, spending eight days in Chile's Patagonia region would have to suffice for us.

The other major activity this day was seeing Vanessa off at the airport for she had to return to Idaho and resume her medical duties as a doctor. It was truly a bummer that she would be missing Easter Island but she vowed to return someday, probably in the Southern winter so she could go skiing in the Andes at the Portillo ski resort and then spend a week on Easter Island.

"I'm not done with this place at all. In the words of the immortal Arnold Schwarzenegger, 'I'll be back,'" Vanessa exclaimed as she hustled off to go through security.

Of course, we were feeling guilty about all of this but then we retreated to our default rationale, namely that we were retired and footloose free. Best of all, there was no change fee from our original airline reservations. So for us, it was off to Punta Arenas tomorrow.

Sunday, Dec 27

The next morning we headed to the airport for our flight to Punta Arenas on Sky Airline, the local, cut-rate airline. This was a small plane, all economy with tight ass seating. Of course, it was packed. To further add to the aggravation, it turned out to be a five-hour flight instead of the scheduled three-and-a-half hours. The reason: an unscheduled stop in the Lake District in which the plane sat on the ground for an hour. No reason given.

But driving was not an option. Since Chile is so long and skinny, it was 1,360 miles (2188 km) from Santiago to Punta Arenas. A long two nights on the road if you are driving.

Nonetheless, we did finally arrive at Punta Arenas, the last major town in Chile on the Straits of Magellan. That in itself was fascinating to me. Just think of it: The Straits of Magellan! A famous shortcut passage of water from the Atlantic to the Pacific. And an often treacherous body of water that sunk god knows how many ships while they tried to traverse it in days of old.

Of course, the actual southernmost point of South America called Cape Horn was about 243 miles further south on the Isla de Tierra Del Fuego which when you looked on a map didn't seem like an island at all but rather part of the South American continent. The main town down there was Ushuaia in Argentina also known as the jumping-off spot for cruise ships to the Antarctic.

Chile's Tip

Upon landing at a small airport with a quonset hut type terminal and securing our luggage, we hiked over to the lone car rental counter that served all the major car rental companies. Guess what? Nobody was on duty. We along with few other tourists milled about, occasionally ringing the bell for service. We could not comprehend that nobody would be here for a major incoming flight even on a Sunday.

By and by, an airport worker sweeping the floor told one of the tourists in Spanish that nobody would be in today at the car rental counter because it was Sunday. Instead, we should take a taxi to the main office in downtown Punta Arenas. That might be open.

"Might be open!" I thought. "What the fuck was going on? Was it a holiday or just South American mañana fever?

Resigned to it, we did hail a taxi. A long row of them were waiting right outside the airport like they were anticipating a bunch of pissed off tourists deprived of their rental cars.

Our cabbie was a nice guy who spoke some English. He explained that this was a common occurrence. On the way to the Europcar rental office, he drove around a picturesque square and pointed out a large statue of Magellan looming over the square. An obvious local hero in these parts.

Actually, the downtown looked rather pleasant and worth exploring later. But for right then, we wanted to get to the rental office. However, as soon as we pulled up, we could see the "Cerrado" sign in the door. So sorry we are closed it said in Spanish. And then I realized it was well past five p.m. but the sun was still blazing as if it was noon.

There was nothing left to do but go on to our hotel which the cabbie was eager to do, no doubt hoping for a big tip which he later got. Minutes later we arrived at the Hotel Isla Rey Jorge.

Hotel Isla Rey Jorge

At first glance, it looked like an old stone mansion from the 19th century but when we entered, it was obvious the place had been renovated. It had a comfortable looking lounge with a fireplace; off to one side was an extensive dining room but the hotel only offered breakfast.

Our room up on the third floor was spacious and still had touches of its old Victorian style. The bathroom featured a large bear claw tub with a shower attachment. Yes, we thought this would do nicely for our several nights here.

Happy and settled at last, we ventured outside a couple of blocks to a modest eating spot. Essentially it was a pizza joint, Mesita Grande, but it served a variety of Italian dishes and featured some great German beer brewed locally. We decided that this would be our favored dining spot. The owner a guy in his mid-thirties had spent several years in New York in the restaurant world and was hip to American tastes in Italian cuisine.

The pizza we ordered did live up to Italian and New York standards. Quite tasty indeed.

When we finished, we went outside and walked around in the still blazing sunlight at nine at night. At first, I thought this was truly the land of the midnight sun. But it wasn't. The sun did eventually set around 10:30 pm. But before it did, we hiked over a few blocks to the waterfront and strolled along a concrete boardwalk fronting the Magellan Strait which was now very placid, gently lapping at the shores of Punta Arenas.

So here we were at last, almost at the bottom of the world and looking forward to the sights and oddities of a Patagonia world.

Monday, Dec. 28

The next morning I was off around nine to pick up my car at the downtown office of Europcar. There I found two guys and a gal lounging around, acting surprised to see a customer so soon. When I presented my Europcar reservation printout, they looked it over very carefully as if to determine its authenticity. Finally, the senior dude explained to me in English that they had no mid-size car available right then but were expecting some soon.

"When is soon?" I asked

"Perhaps around noon or one."

Not wanting to wait around, I replied, "Well let me see what you do have available right now. A compact might do."

"Si, Senor."

And with that, he led me out of the office to a little Renault parked on the street. It looked quite old and dowdy but serviceable. When I indicated that I would take it, the guy pointed out that it had no radio. And indeed when I looked more closely, there was a gaping hole in the dashboard where the radio had been. No doubt stolen.

The guy then assured me that while the car might not look like much, it was very reliable and ran well.

"O.K. If you say so," I replied with visions of being broken down on some lonely road waiting for the triple-A tow truck to arrive. Still, I didn't want to wait a half-day. We had plans to see a popular sight around here, a penguin breeding ground. So I signed up for the car rationalizing that I could trade it in later in the day if it misbehaved.

Surprisingly, as I drove it around the town, I discovered that it did drive very well and I decided I could live without a radio. But I did vow to email Europcar headquarters that they should fire their whole staff at the office for dereliction of their rental car duties.

I returned to the hotel and picked up Yvonne for our excursion to see some penguins. This was being touted as a must thing to do while in Punta Arenas. Now, Yvonne and I have seen many penguins in various zoos, small penguins, large penguins and penguins in-between so I wondered what the big deal was. The answer always was, "You must see them in their natural habitat."

So it was we headed out town about eighty kilometers to the Parque Pinguino Del Seno Otway situated on an inlet from the strait. But after driving over a long and bumpy gravel road we were greeted with a sign that said the park was closed today.

"Shit, shit, shit. What are the penguins on strike or what?" I ranted. No, according to an unread passage in my guidebook, the park was sometimes closed depending on weather, time of day, holidays or just because. After all, this was still Latin America.

On our drive back along the strait, we did notice a bunch of parked cars at a small ferry terminal with a sign promoting the penguins of Isla Magdalena. We had considered this option before but it required taking an all-day tour to the small island off the strait to see some king penguins. It was on this islet that penguins were said to congregate to lay eggs and such. The only problem was we hadn't scheduled a day for that. And anyway, we felt at this point, why bother. We were down here to see much more impressive sights.

So we continued heading back toward town, stopping at various points with stunning views of the Magellan Strait.

Magellan Strait

At one viewpoint, we could see the tantalizing Isla Tierra del Fuego off in the distance and we wondered if we had made a mistake by not including it in our itinerary. Probably.

Not giving up on our tour of the Punta Arenas region, we passed through town and kept heading south out onto the Brunswick Peninsula. Here, the landscape became more picturesque with the strait glittering off in the distance and forested hills lining the coast similar to the lush forests of the Olympic Peninsula.

Our paved road soon turned to gravel but we drove on to our goal, Cabo Froward, the southernmost point of the continental Americas and one of my major goals for this trip.

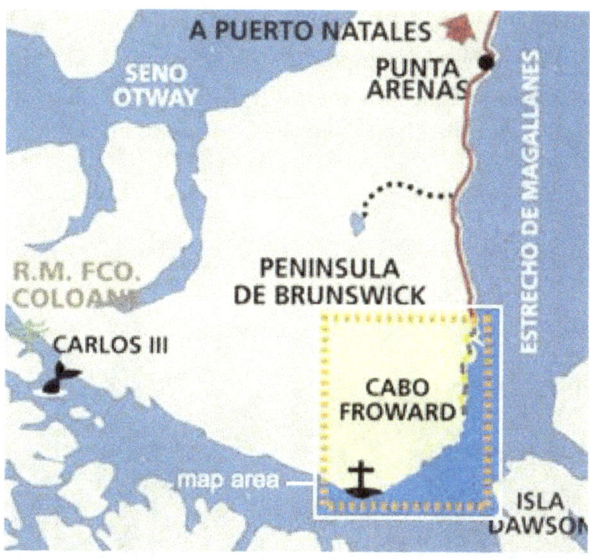

A glance at a map of this region is confusing because the Magellan Strait cuts off a large portion of landmasses that are technically islands (i.e. Tierra del Fuego) which continue south for several hundred miles. Further, there is a dispute as to whether a continent can or cannot include nearby islands. However, for our purposes and as the signs declared, Cabo Froward on the Brunswick Peninsula was the end of the road for the American continents.

Cabo Froward

Actually, to reach the physical southernmost point, you have to hike onto a butt of land where a large metal cross that marked the actual point. We decided to forego that and merely take a short walk along a gravel beach while gazing at the strait from the Cabo Froward area.

Capo Froward Point

Mission accomplished we turned around and headed back to Punta Arenas, stopping here and there to take pictures of some fascinating shipwrecks.

Shipwrecks

It was a real nautical junkyard just sitting there, some of it fenced off. I guess they were saving the wrecks for parts or maybe for a complete restoration or maybe for nothing. Maybe the locals were just too lazy to clean up the mess. Who knew?

We didn't return to Punta Arenas until late afternoon. Tired from our day of exploration and futile hunt for penguins, we chilled for a while and then returned to our chosen restaurant, Mesita Grande.

Tuesday, Dec. 29

We spent most of the morning visiting local museums. First up was the Museo Regional de Magallanes. Housed in an opulent mansion, this museum had extensive displays on the lifestyle of the rich pioneer sheep farmers in the late 19th century. Room after room was filled with elaborate examples of Victorian salons. The museum also had a section on the local flora and fauna, the history of native tribes in this area as well as a display of the bones and hairy skin of the now-extinct Mylodon. The Mylodon was a giant ice age sloth that roamed this area more than 10-thousand years ago.

Regional Museum of Magellan

Mylodon Sloth

After we got done with this museum, we checked out the main plaza of Punta Arenas which was right across the street. While it was a picturesque plaza with all the prerequisite trees, shrubbery and winding pathways, the main attraction here was a statue of Ferdinand Magellan, the 16th century Portuguese explorer who discovered the Magellan Strait in 1520 on his around the world voyage.

Ferdinand Magellan

Undaunted and diseased and with the constant threat of mutiny, Magellan successfully made his way through the strait which if you look at the map, you will note the strait is not very straight at all but rather filled with narrow, twisting passages and small islands clogging the route. Add to that the constant stormy waters of the strait and you have quite a feat of navigation for a 16th century sailing ship.

Map Magellan Strait

Following a leisurely walk around the plaza, we hiked over a few blocks to the Museo Naval y Maritimo, documenting the rich maritime history of the area.

Nautical Museum

Here was display after display of various nautical bric-a-brac and descriptions of Chilean naval history. A lot of the exhibit focused on Cape Horn and the Antarctic. It was said that they kept a chunk of ice from the Antarctic in a case below freezing but either we didn't see it or notice it if it was actually on display. What we did notice was a spectacular film of a sailing ship rounding Cape Horn during a storm, a film by Irving Johnson shot in the early in the 20th century. All in all, this museum gave us a sense of the challenges and the drama of seafaring in this place.

Done with the nautical museum, we continued on. While walking down one street, we heard and saw something rather odd—a storefront radio station called Radio Polar. From what we could make out from its outdoor speakers, it was broadcasting in a language that was definitely not Spanish. More like some east European language. Plus there was a sign in Spanish and English and Croatian. Croatian?

Checking on-line later, I discovered that Punta Arenas had a large Croatian population. Thousands had emigrated here starting in the early 20th century. Who knew?

Radio Polar

But then as noted earlier, many non-Spanish speaking European groups had settled in Chile in addition to the Germans. Brits, Basque, whomever. Also, the Croatians had produced many notable business people, politicians and sports figures. Chile was indeed a surprising melting pot.

***

Later that evening, we skipped dining at Mesita Grande and ate at a recommended high-end fish restaurant called La Luna. It was a busy, crowded place with snotty waiters. At first, we had to wait for a table and then we were seated at one long table with other diners. Across from us was a young British woman traveling alone. We introduced ourselves and started chit-chatting while waiting for our food. It turned that Margaret worked for an American agricultural firm in Britain. Somehow we got on the subject of genetically modified food. She explained how GMOs were slowly invading Europe despite anti-GMO regulations.

I asked how they got around that.

"It's simple enough. They simply put the GMO in animal feed. No restrictions there."

That was disillusioning but she was a charmer and when I asked how come she was on her own here. She answered. "She, who travels alone, travels the swiftest." And then she added that she had just concluded a small group trek through the Torres Del Paine region.

A real independent spirit. But not too different from our daughter Vanessa who had completed a similar small group trek.

Oh, by the way, the so-called specialty of the house which we had was a lobster dish. Alas, it was mediocre and certainly not worth the price we paid. It was back to the pizza parlor for us for the rest of our stay in Punta Arenas.

7. TORRES DEL PAINE

Wednesday, Dec. 30

Early the next morning we bid goodbye to Punta Arenas and hit the road for Puerto Natales about 248 kilometers north on Highway 9, the only road around. Puerto Natales is the main gateway town to the much-vaunted Torres del Paine National Park. We were going to base ourselves in Natales for the next three nights.

Driving along we discovered that the scenery was pretty boring, mostly flat scrubland with no mountains in sight but

there were a lot of colorful lupines flowers along the roadside so we stopped and snapped a few photos of them.

Lupines

By and by, we reached the outskirts of Puerto Natales, which at first appearance struck us as rather junky. The downtown was a bit better but lined with tourist excursion agencies all with signs screaming for your business.

Puerto Natales

We did note that the town was situated on the shores of what appeared to us to be a lake but later learned that it was an inlet of the Ultima Esperanza Sound. This sound which led to hundreds of fjords all of which ultimately drained into the Pacific Ocean.

Ultima Esperanza Sound

During our drive through downtown, we saw scores of young people all loaded down with gigantic backpacks boarding buses which were most likely headed to Torres del Paine. From what we could see, all were outfitted with the proper hiking boots and the requisite breakaway hiking pants.

As the afternoon was waning, we decided to check into our hotel on the outskirts of town. While searching for it, we encountered a pack of dogs that seem to be bent on some destination, probably a feeding event.

Dog Pack

After taking a few wrong turns, we finally came across the Hotel Doble E Patagonia. It was billed as a so-called echo lodge but for this time of year, the price seemed reasonable. One hundred dollars a night in the high summer season. It had a pleasant setting with a lot of grounds. Inside it was very nicely laid out. The rooms looked quite comfortable and it had a large lounge and eating area. Of course, breakfast was included. All in all, quite a homey looking place.

Hotel Doble E Patagonia

We hung around the hotel for a while, having a beer in the lounge and chatting with a retired German couple who had just arrived too. They were on a tour of the entire South American continent but we did talk about Germany. Both said they were retired just in time because Germany was about to raise its retirement age to 65. Right then it was several years lower. They also bitched about the flood of Middle East immigrants coming in.

"Germany has enough foreigners," the Herr proclaimed. "The government should go back to the old enforceable borders and also back to the Mark while they are at it. If Chancellor Merkel doesn't watch out the right-wing is going to take over."

So much for international relations.

After that little conversation, we went out for dinner. Not wanting a big deal, we found a food truck in a supermarket parking lot with delicious Chilean tortilla sandwiches. We added fries to this repast and had yet another beer. Day one in Puerto Natales was over. Tomorrow Torres del Paine.

Thursday, Dec 31

This was the day for one of our major destinations of the whole trip —Torres del Paine or loosely translated into English "Towers of Blue." So it was with eager anticipation that we got an early start after partaking of a filling breakfast at the hotel. As we got going, I realized that our journey would not be long as we sped north on the main route to the park. In fact, it was only sixty kilometers into the southern entrance, most of it on paved road. About halfway along the mountains started to come into view. Beautiful, craggy mountains many with lakes at their base.

But as soon as we entered the park, the road turned to gravel. Supposedly, this was an effort to keep the environment natural but it was annoying as gravel kept pinging the undersides of our rental.

South Entrance

As we drove along on this gravel road, I had to admit these mountains were stunning and dramatic but I have seen similar scenes before. This southern part of the park reminded me of the Grand Tetons of Wyoming and the Colorado San Juans all wrapped up as one.

About a half-hour into the park, we stopped at one scenic spot for a short hike along a designated hiking path. Unfortunately, we had lots of company. The parking lot was packed with tour buses and hikers crowded the trail. Still, despite the unusual heat, it was pleasant with the stunning views of the mountains, some with glaciers and rushing streams of rapids. We spent an hour gazing around here before we moved on.

Rapids

Driving on, we started getting views of what Torres del Paine is rightly famous for—the near-vertical rock towers of up to nine thousand feet. They made for a spectacular, awe-inspiring sight. Vanessa had told us her group had hiked around the base of one such tower even ascending a few hundred feet up it but bad weather moved in and they called the mini-climb off.

Torres del Paine

A few miles farther on, we stopped at Hotel Del Torres located at the base of one group of towers. This old line hotel which was once a ranch house looked kind of funky and slightly rundown to me but it was the "in" place to stay for exploring the towers of Torres Del Paine. Of course, it was expensive, about $400.00 a day.

Hotel Las Torres

We parked and went inside the hotel but could barely make our way through the crowded lobby filled with would-be, hikers, all of many ages, some even looking to be in their 80s. Most were fully geared up and looking ready to conquer the towers.

Out back, we noticed that a hiking tour was moving off to the base of the towers. Actually, few people scale these towers. Such a feat is limited to highly experienced rock and mountain climbers. I would guess that somebody who has scaled El Capitan in Yosemite might be able to do it.

More Towers

After we were here an hour or so, we moved on, taking a short-cut out of the park feeling that we had seen what one could see in a day. Of course, we had seen only a fraction of the park although we had seen the most spectacular part.

The best way to see it all is to hike the Circuit Trail of some 110 kilometers like Vanessa did. This required a week of hiking and staying in huts along the way. But alas, there was no way we old farts were going to do that.

We felt satisfied that had seen what we did and glad for our little hike. But in the last analysis, we thought that while Torres del Paine was worth seeing, it should be supplemented with other Patagonia sights to make a trip down here worthwhile.

On our drive out of the park, we ran into herd after herd of guanacos. They look like llamas but are only remotely related. They were everywhere, including standing on the road and barely moving out of our way. These critters were the size of small horses with long necks and said to be the ancestors of today's llamas. Also, we noticed that the dominant male liked to stand like a sentinel on rocky points as protector of the herds. Annoying but fascinating.

Guanacos

Sentinel

As we emerged from the national park, we drove by a sign indicating a turn off to Argentina. Argentina! Yes. At this point in Chile, the border to Argentina was only a few kilometers away. I was tempted to check it out but remembered Vanessa's warning that it could take hours to cross the border because Argentina was constantly in a dispute with Chile over the exact border location down here in Patagonia. So basically from out of spite, the border guards made it tough for Chileans and anyone else to cross over. O.K. so we forgot the border crossing and drove on.

Actually, the most interesting sight that we saw on our drive back to Port Natales was a sign on the highway that indicated that we were indeed at the end of the world. Ruta del Fin del Mundo. What better way to end our day of exploration.

Oh, I almost forgot, this was New Year's Eve but for the life of me, I can't remember what we did to celebrate so stoked we were on the day's events. Probably nothing other than a few beers with some other guests as we said goodbye to 2015.

Friday, January 1, 2016

New Year's Day shone bright and warm in Puerto Natales. After another leisurely breakfast, we headed out to visit a cave. Not just any cave but the Mylodon Cave Natural Monument about twenty kilometers northwest of Puerto Natales.

This cave was said to be full of bones and tools from human habitation from about eleven thousand years ago. The bones were those of the giant sloth-like creature, the Mylodon, the saber tooth tiger and a camel-like creature.

Since this was a holiday, I was afraid that the tourists would be out in force at the cave but when we arrived the parking lot was empty. Good.

We parked and hiked over to the entrance to the cave. Nobody was around and admission was apparently free today since nobody was in the little ticket booth. In other words, the cave was open to anyone who showed up.

Mylodon Cave

Inside we followed a path that looped through the musty interior of the cave which was about two hundred yards long and almost a football field wide. It also had a soaring hundred-foot ceiling. Walking through this massive cave was like visiting a primordial Chartres Cathedral. While we were in the middle of this cave trek, I had this eerie feeling that I could smell the former inhabitants, as if they had just left for a hunting expedition. I felt I could even sense their spirits, spooky but inspiring.

The various points of interest were marked with archeological dig pits and signs explaining what had once been here. This along with a sculpture of a giant Mylodon. However, we saw no bones or tools from that period nor any hairy patches of fur. All that had been removed to various museums like the one we had seen in Punta Arenas.

The American Museum of Natural History in New York apparently had a full-size skeleton of a Mylodon sloth to give you an idea of its size.

Mylodon Skeleton

After a couple of hours of doing the cave thing, we returned to Puerto Natales and drove through downtown looking for somewhere to eat lunch but every restaurant we saw was closed until we came upon a pizza parlor off on a side street that was full of people. So we entered and ordered pizza and beer. The pizza finally arrived after we had downed most of our beer. Yvonne said the pizza was the best she had ever tasted, even better than our eatery in Punta Arenas. I had to agree. Imagine that the best pizza in the world was to be had at the end of the world.

Following lunch and in order to work off the beer and pizza, we strolled up and down the main street. Sure enough, as already mentioned, most of the businesses were indeed closed except for a few travel agencies touting cruises on the sound and up into the fjords where, as the signs proclaimed, you could see glaciers coming right down to the water.

We had been planning to do this all along but I had not made advance reservations so I figured it was time to sign up for a tour for tomorrow if possible. So we entered one such agency called Turismo 21 de Mayo.

The guy on duty was very accommodating and very quick at extracting our 300-dollars via credit card. He explained that we were lucky to find such a cruise on such short notice.

He described in glowing terms the sights we would see from the boat, plus a couple of short excursions on foot. In addition, at extra cost, another hundred dollars, they offered zodiac trips at some of these destinations to further round out the trip. I bit and signed up for a zodiac trip.

"There is absolutely no way to see these wonderful attractions except by taking a boat and a zodiac tour," he exclaimed. "There are no roads or trails into these remote areas."

He further explained the boat was luxurious with free drinks and snacks. Also included was a big meal stopover at one remote sheep ranch. It all sounded enticing and maybe worth the four-hundred dollars I had just spent. We would see.

Following this bit of business, we returned to our hotel and relaxed for the rest of the day.

Saturday, Jan. 2

The next morning, bright and early we were at the waterfront boarding one of the Turismo 21 de Mayo excursion boats. It was a nice craft with a lot of seating in the interior and big picture windows. There wasn't a lot of space topside for the passengers but nobody much cared because it was blustery and cold. Once underway, the crew started passing out hot apple cider with a splash of rum. Hey, this might be all right!

Excursion Boat

So we settled back and watched the scenery go by which at this point was mainly the choppy sound and a few distant mountains. Still, it was hard to believe that the Ultima Esperanza Sound was not a lake but rather an offshoot of the Magellan Strait. Of course, I knew there was quite a difference from a lake and a sound, the main one being this sound was a body of saltwater and a lake was comprised of freshwater.

Esperanza Sound

Meanwhile swooping black cormorants were busy dive-bombing our boat as we chugged along. About a half-hour into our voyage, we came upon our first fjord featuring a narrow waterfall. It was rather nice but not especially exciting.

Narrow Waterfall

When most people think of fjords, they think of Norway but really, fjords can be found in all shapes and sizes throughout the world such as in Alaska, New Zealand and here in Patagonia.

Moving on, we eventually came upon what we were most interested in: Fjords with glaciers coming right down into the water. At one point, the boat docked and we hiked along a short path to examine a couple of the more spectacular glaciers, the Balmaceda and Serrano glaciers.

Balmaceda Glacier

Serrano Glacier

After twenty minutes or so here taking pictures, we returned to the boat and cruised by several more similar sights but then the boat paused at a spot where we were supposed to board zodiacs for a closer looked at the glaciers. I looked out and all I could see was a lot of chop and a high wind whistling over the waters.

Really, did we want to get into a rubbery, twisty zodiac and chance these waters?

Up front of the boat, the crew was quietly conferring and after a few minutes of scanning the water, they announced that it was too rough for a zodiac outing and that we would be refunded for the extra cost of such a venture. O.K. that was good for us. We were in no mood to battle the watery elements from a low slung zodiac that could easily fill with water and possibly sink.

Just minutes after the announcement, the crew came by with shot glasses and Irish whiskey for us to have a snort. If we wanted a hot drink, apple cider with rum was still available at the bar. All gratis of course.

At this point, the boat turned around and we headed up another inlet flanked by low rolling hills, almost pasture like.

And indeed they were pastures, sheep pastures as it turned out for we were passing through the grounds of a large sheep ranch.

By and by, we pulled up at a dock and disembarked.

The guides led us up a path to a rambling farm house with a large canopied patio. Underneath the canopy scores of tables and chairs set up. It was a rather festive atmosphere with a live band playing Chilean folk music. This was where we were going to dine for lunch huddled down in our parkas since the wind was still whipping.

We all took our seats and waited for the feed to begin. We happened to be sitting next to a couple from Canberra, Australia who was touring Patagonia with their daughter, an exchange student on scholarship at the University of Santiago. The senior was an economist for the Australian Government. We chit-chatted a bit while we waited for our meal.

Talking about Chilean society, the daughter said she had observed that Chileans are usually a close-knit group, very family-oriented and cold to outsiders and that this was probably the result of years of Pinochet rule where with the wrong word said to the wrong person, you could disappear in the middle of the night.

Based on our tour of the Memory museum, I wasn't about to dispute that. Despite this negative appraisal, she claimed she had a Chilean boyfriend and was having a grand time in Chile.

As we talked I discovered that Australia and Chile had rather close links in the areas of trade, foreign aid and defense. I guess it was part of the brotherhood of the Southern Hemisphere. But when you think about it made sense in view of recent incursions by the Chinese and Russians who are trying to gain influence in the southern hemisphere. The Southern Hemisphere with its vital oceanic passages such as the Straits of Magellan would be a prize for that pair.

However, so far, the major powers of the southern hemisphere including Australia and New Zealand all have defense links with Chile along with the U.S. Indeed President Barak Obama had set up two U.S. military installations in Chile, one near Valparaiso. Their stated mission was to collect intelligence and also provide humanitarian relief in case of various disasters that befall Chile such as earthquakes.

Back on the subject of today's cruise, I said it reminded me of the fjords on South Island, New Zealand. The Aussies concurred with that.

"Yes, yes," the mister agreed. But you know I find Patagonia much more exotic and interesting than the South Island of New Zealand. Apart from the coastal mountains and the ever diminishing glaciers, it's all rather boring."

"Yes, I agree," interjected Yvonne. "Boring but charming. Rather like visiting grandmother's house."

"Well, put," said the mother. "Oz is far more dynamic. And god knows we have thousands of Kiwis coming to our shores to work and enjoy higher pay and a better lifestyle."

By this time our meal had arrived. It consisted of large chunks of mutton, boiled potatoes and sides of various vegetables. Also free beer and a bottle of wine for each table.

Now, Yvonne and I often have Australian lamb at home that we buy at Costco. It is tender, juicy and delicious.

But this was mutton from an older sheep and one bite was enough to tell me it was of a whole different order and not a good one. It was tough, dry with a lot of fatty parts. This sheep must have been almost dead. I managed to gag down several chunks, one with a bone in it that I ate caveman style. Eventually, I gave up and filled up with the potatoes and veggies, all washed down by beer.

The Aussie family remarked that this was certainly not the best mutton that they had ever tasted but that dining on mutton was quite common in Australia.

"Not lamb?" I interjected.

"Rarely. We hardly ever have lamb because it's so expensive."

"I don't know. It's pretty cheap at Costco and delicious too," I replied.

"Yes, well you know all the great cuts of meat including lamb are shipped abroad so you Yanks can dine well. We get to eat the leavings unless we are willing to pay top price."

End of lamb conversation.

It was also the end of the meal. It was time to re-board the boat and head back to Puerto Natales in what was now a raging storm with wind and sleet making several passengers seasick. But an hour later or so we were back in port safe and sound. We returned to our hotel and stayed put there for the rest of the evening while the storm raged outside. Middle of summer in the Southern Hemisphere! Say what!

This postscript: The promised refund for the canceled zodiac excursion never came through at first. In fact, the tour agency had double charged me for the whole tour. What the fuck!

It was only after I refused to pay the charge on my credit card and then explained the situation to American Express that they got on the case with Turismo 21 de Mayo. A month later, the double charge was reduced to one and included a refund for the zodiac excursion.

8. FORT & PENGUINS

Sunday, Jan. 3

Nothing much going on. We just drove back to Punta Arenas and checked into our hotel, Hotel Isla Rey Jorge. Tiring of pizza, we had some great lasagna at our default restaurant and then walked around the plaza a bit in the evening.

Alas, the plaza was now filled with teenagers with boom boxes pounding out rap. Many were on skateboards zooming around the statue of Magellan, making it unsafe to walk through the area. All in all, it gave us and probably Magellan a headache and we returned to the hotel.

Oh, yes, the only major decision of the day was to forgo a tour to Tierra del Fuego to an area where the king penguins roamed. It involved taking a ferry across the strait to the town of Porvenir on the north coast and then a long ride over bumpy, unpaved roads in a crowded van with a tour guide at the hefty price of 350-dollars per couple.

Still feeling duty-bound to see at least a few penguins in Patagonia, we decided to go back to Seno Otway park late afternoon the next day when the penguins supposedly came out to feed. According to the hotel manager, the park was now open on a Monday afternoon.

Monday, Jan 4

Since we were not going to Seno Otway park until late afternoon, we decided to drive down the Brunswick Peninsula again to look for an old fort that we had missed on our first go-around of the area. This was the Feurte Bulnes, a fortress built by the Chilean army in the mid-19th century.

The problem was it was hard to find. There was virtually no signage to point the way to the fort that I could see. Eventually, we did find the turn off which took us out onto another point of land called Punta Santa Ana. And there in the distance, we could make out the barricade fence surrounding the fort.

We parked in the dirt lot and then took a path leading up to the fort which was actually a restored version of the original fort. The restoration included a church, a jail, a post office, stables, a powder magazine and a couple of cannons pointing out to sea.

Cannons

By way of background, Fuerte Bulnes was founded in 1843 by the Chileans to protect the Strait of Magellan. At the time, various other nations including France and Britain were challenging Chile for control of the strait. So with this fort and plenty of cannon on a point, Chile laid final claim to its southern territories and Patagonia. The fort was kind of interesting but rather familiar. It reminded me of the Russian fort on the northern California coast, Fort Ross, that I had seen many, many times.

Later that day after a stopover for lunch at Punta Arenas, we headed out once again to find those fuck'n penguins. As noted before this involved a fifty-mile drive, fifteen of it over a rutted gravel road to get to Seno Otway Park.

We arrived at the park around four. We pulled into the parking lot, got out of the car and were practically blown away.

Dust and debris were flying everywhere. To make matters worse the penguin viewing area was a good hundred yards away in this windstorm.

Seno Otway Park

Undeterred, we trudged on over to the shores of the inlet and joined a small crowd observing a couple of dozen penguins. Overall, these were not an impressive lot, small by even penguin standards and all they did was waddle around, pecking here and there at various edible items on the beach. Of course, they ignored the onlookers who were crowding in on the viewing platform to take pictures.

Unimpressive Penguins

We listened in on a tour director of a small group lecturing on the lifestyle of the penguins. It was nothing that I hadn't heard before. Indeed, I had gotten a lot more out of the movie March of the Penguins narrated by the voice-of-god actor Morgan Freeman a few years ago.

I soon got bored and tired of the high wind with all the sand particles sandblasting my face so I returned to the car. Yvonne forged on farther down the beach seeing even more penguins while I sat in the car, warm and cozy and read.

***

That night, our last night in Punta Arenas, while dining again at our pizza spot, Mesita Grande, we assessed our feelings about the place. Actually, we rather liked Punta Arenas. It was not pretentious and not overly touristy like Puerto Natales. It was just a commercial town sitting on the Magellan Strait with some interesting attractions. Best of all the Chileans here were not overactive, screamers, probably because most were descended from non-Hispanic European countries.

We were also especially taken by the scores of American millennials in their late twenties or thirties trekking here in full Abercrombie hiking gear and spending lots of dough. As one put it at our hotel in Puerto Natales, "I am going to blow it all traveling."

"But what about saving for a rainy day?" I asked.

The common refrain response was, "Hey, I expect to work until I drop dead because, as far as I can see social security will be bankrupt and of course there will be no pensions except for my 401 K which I plan to start on when I get back."

"Good show."

Oh, to be young again.

On the other hand, there were several older singles trekking around here. One was a live-wire woman who looked very fit but who was probably in her mid-70s. We encountered Angela while lounging and drinking beer in the Puerto Natales hotel. She had just been on an Antarctic tour before trekking Torres del Paine. I wanted to know all about her trip because I felt guilty that we missed something by not doing the Antarctic.

I mean here we were only a few hundred miles from a popular jumping-off point for cruise ships going to Antarctica. But I also knew a cruise to Antarctica was god awful expensive. But as this spitfire put it:

"It needn't be. There are relatively cheap ways of doing it. Not being on a schedule, I flew down to Ushuaia, Argentina on the tip of Cape Horn and waited for the right cruise ship to come along. Of course, it happened to be a Russian cruise/freighter that came along with plenty of vacant berths. It wasn't luxurious but it was cheap."

"If you don't mind me asking, how cheap?"

"About seven thousand for a ten-day cruise."

"Really, so what did you see?"

"Well, we landed on the Antarctic peninsula that juts way out from the main continent. We were in kayaks paddling around marveling at the icy landscape and all the birds, the whales and of course the penguins. We did go onshore and walk around getting a close look at the giant Emperor penguins. Actually, they were kind of friendly and very accepting of humans but basically, they just ignored us. And went about their business."

"Did you ever get to the mainland?"

"No, not really. We viewed it from afar. It was like another planet, an ice planet."

She went on to explain that most of the luxury cruise ships don't do much more than that and then charge double of what she paid. Only rarely do the cruise ships visit the coastal stations on the mainland.

"So do you think it was worth the seven grand you paid?" I inquired.

"As I said, that was a bargain price and yes, it was well worth it for me, a poor retired school teacher from San Francisco. It was a once in a lifetime experience."

So there it was. Perhaps a missed opportunity.

9. EASTER ISLAND

Tuesday, Jan 5

We flew back to Santiago and checked into our Hilton purgatory for two more nights until our "maybe" flight to Easter Island on the 7th. Still, rumors of another LAN strike were circulating in the news. We will see what is what in two days. If this effort falls through we will say "fuck it" and fly home directly. So much for Easter Island.

Wednesday, Jan 6

Basically, we chilled at the hotel, dining, downing Piscos Sours and lounging in the rooftop pool. Late afternoon we got word from the receptionist that a strike had been avoided. LAN and LAN management had reached an agreement. I guess one strike over the Christmas holidays was enough for both parties.

Thursday, Jan 7

So what do you know? We are actually flying to Easter Island this morning. The airport was as usual, a pig fuck. The check-in line to the LAN Easter Island flight was long. It seemed like everyone had three or four suitcases, a large screen TV and a couple of appliance boxes. One family even had a freezer on a roller. I surmised that these were actual residents of Easter Island. Many had the pure Polynesian looks.

Eventually, we made it to the head of the line and checked in, no sweat. Then we boarded what appeared to be a brand new Boeing Dreamliner. It was slick and even our economy seats were roomy. This along with a sophisticated entertainment center and some great cuisine made our six-hour flight to Easter Island go by fast.

"What, a six-hour flight, you say!" That's what I thought when I first heard about it but then checking the mileage the distance from Santiago, Chile to Easter Island I discovered that it was about the same as from San Francisco to Hawaii, around 2,350 miles. So the flight times were similar.

Along the way, I mentally reviewed all the fantasies that I had had about Easter Island since I was a kid. The first one was based on a Disney comic book that followed the adventures of Uncle Scrooge and his exploits with his nephews, Huey, Louie and Dewey, while looking for treasure on Easter Island.

Then there was Wonder Woman and various other superheroes tangling with the mysterious moai statues.

I also remembered one comic that had Superman flying to Easter Island to ascertain if the moai statues had been planted by beings from another planet, possibly his home planet, Krypton.

Finally, over the years I recalled that Easter Island had been a source of comic inspiration in cartoons, magazines and newspapers such as this one by John Deering.

In addition to seeing many documentaries on Easter Island and the origin of the statues littering its landscape, I had read Norwegian Explorer Thor Heyerdahl's first book on his 1955 expedition to Easter Island—"Aku Aku: The Secret of Easter Island."

This was a fascinating read about the current archeology of the time and Heyerdahl's theory that the first Easter Islanders came from South America, not Polynesia. An idea that still hangs around today despite genetic proof that the first islanders were indeed Polynesian. More about this later.

***

Thus it was after six hours of flying over an empty blue Pacific, we landed on the most isolated island in the world, Easter Island or as it is officially known "Rapa Nui."

The airport was a madhouse when we landed but once we procured our luggage a nice Polynesian lady from our car rental agency was there with our rental car. Good thing too because we needed a guide to find our hotel, the Taja Tai. You see Hanga Roa is the main and only town on the island and while not large, its layout is a maze with no street signs and it would have been hard to figure out without this lady.

As soon as we arrived at the hotel, we said goodbye to the nice lady who had her own car in the parking lot and proceeded to check-in. The setting was great for this hotel. It had extensive tropical gardens and right out back great views of the ocean. The wood-paneled rooms were comfortable looking with king-size beds. But best of all there was a large pool at hand which we immediately took advantage of.

Taja Tai Hotel

We scrambled to get our bathing suits on and into the pool. Later, we relaxed on a recliner in the shade with a tall Mai Tai at our side. We felt as if we were back in Tahiti many long years ago because everything we had seen so far reminded us of Polynesia, the people, the town and the general laid-back feeling.

About the only difference here from a typical Polynesian island was the rocky, landscape and the absence of lush, green vegetation except where it had been purposely planted.

Following our swim, we returned to our room and then went out around 6 p.m.to look for dinner. First, we checked out the dining room menu and found it quite expensive even if it did have a spectacular view of the Pacific.

Then, I remembered spotting a ramshackle restaurant across the road that looked like it was constructed of driftwood. Yvonne and I thought that it looked interesting. I mean how bad it could be being so close to the hotel? We trudged on over to the Mamma Nui restaurant and checked out the menu posted at the entrance. For the same fish dinner that the hotel was offering, the price was about half.

Mamma Nui Restaurant

So we sat down at a table under an outdoor canopy with a pleasant breeze blowing. We decided on the spot to have dinner here along with a couple of beers. Our waiter was, in fact, the owner, a nice Chilean guy who said he had moved here several years ago and married a local Polynesian gal. So he was now a true Easter Islander. The fish dinner with sides was great. I don't know how the hotel cuisine could have been any better.

Following dinner, we walked around, up and down the main road in the sunset. All was quiet, all was peaceful. A stray dog came sniffing by, looking for food and not at all aggressive. After that, it was back to our room where we watched some local Easter Island TV in Spanish and forthwith crashed.

Friday, Jan 8

During breakfast the next morning, we debated how to best tackle this island with its mysterious moai. We ultimately decided that before we checked out the various moai sites we should arm ourselves with more information and background about the Easter Islanders. From reading and watching documentaries, we already knew quite a lot about Easter Island.

We knew that about 800 AD, Polynesian voyagers from what is now French Polynesia crossed the open sea in gigantic double-hulled canoes, most likely stocked with foodstuffs and possibly animals looking for a new homeland. They eventually found it on Easter Island which at that time was heavily forested and had a potentially rich agricultural environment.

Then after several hundred years due to overpopulation and depletion of resources like timber, different tribal factions went to war with each other and pretty much wiped each other out by the time the Europeans arrived in the early 18th century. Of course, they left behind their giant statues, many in a half-completed state, the exact purpose of which remains a mystery today.

O.K. that was the general picture. But we wanted to find out the specific details at the local museum, the Padre Sebastian Englert Museum.

Following a little map of Hanga Roa that the hotel gave us, we drove over to the museum on the other edge of town.

Housed in a low slung building supposedly resembling an ancient Easter Island dwelling, we entered its portals and were greeted by a young man on the admission desk. We paid a small entrance fee and then browsed around. The museum was filled with many explanatory signs in both Spanish and English.

Hanga Roa Museum

On display were stone tools, wooden kava bowls, a statue representing a woman and pieces of wood with symbols that have yet to be deciphered. These were the mysterious rongo-rongo writings. Perhaps some sort of pictograph writing.

Rongo-Rongo Writing

Several signs described the traditional society, the architecture and the customs of the Easter Islanders. One, in particular, noted the importance of tattoos.

All very informative but the museum avoided the controversial practices of the inhabitants in their later years such as the waring feuds, cannibalism and the cutting down of all the trees which resulted in not being able to construct double-hull canoes to escape from the island.

We did groove on one moai head which cast a dark primitive spirit with its hypnotic deep eye sockets.

Moai Head

There were also charts illustrating the probable voyages of the Easter Islanders in their heyday including voyages to South America.

We struck up a conversation with the 20-something kid at the desk who spoke excellent English and was very bright. We asked how come the Easter Islanders came close to starving in their later years. He answered that they had overexploited their resources and that the fishing was lousy for a period of time. Further, they never brought their domestic pigs along for breeding when they first voyaged here because they ate too much.

"What about the sweet potatoes found here? They are not native to Polynesia," I asked.

"That's right," he replied. "They came from South America."

"So there was contact with South America."

"Yes. Plenty of contact with South America. You know that Polynesian DNA was found in what is now Brazil and Polynesian artifacts have been discovered on the islands near Antarctica."

"Wow! Small world," I remarked.

After that little conversation, we had enough of the museum and headed out of town to explore more of the island.

We drove south towards Orongo Park, one of the main attractions of Easter Island. This park featured a mile-wide crater of an extinct volcano, Rano Kau. In the center of the crater was a lake, really a freshwater swamp that once provided figs and other edible goodies for the Easter Islanders along with trees for firewood.

Rano Kau Crater

We stood on the rim and gazed at the crater for quite a while and then hiked a half-mile or so along a path on the rim for more spectacular views of the surrounding countryside as well as the Pacific Ocean.

Following our look at the crater, we moved on to the nearby village of Orongo which was once the ceremonial center for a birdman cult which I will go into later. There we viewed a restored collection of low, sod-covered stone dwellings with no windows and sunken doors. We also saw burial pits and the stone ceremonial platforms called ahus.

Orongo Village

Kind of creepy and claustrophobic, I thought. We wandered around here for a while and then hiked back along the path to where we were parked.

Along the way, we spotted a tiny rock island a few hundred yards or so from the mainland. A sign at a viewpoint told us that this islet, Motu Nui, was the famous destination of the birdman cult.

Bird Island

Here's how that went. This defining ritual was an annual race to bring the first sooty tern egg back undamaged from the islet to Orongo. It was a very dangerous race because it involved diving or climbing down a cliff face and then swimming out to the islet in shark-infested waters. Many swimmers met their fate in the jaws of sharks.

But whoever made it first to the islet had to procure the fragile egg, put it into a small basket and then signal that he had the egg. Then after a period of fasting, the apparent winner would have to swim back through the shark-infested water and climb up the cliff, still not cracking the egg. He who succeeded in doing all of this was treated like royalty for a year and showered with rewards. Of course, the basis for this exercise was to prove your manhood peacefully instead of going to war.

Following Orongo, we drove over to a nearby area called Ahu Vinapu. It was here that we saw a wall of stones that were perfectly fitted together. This indicated a level of stone masonry that seemed to be inspired by the Incas of Peru. Perhaps lending a degree of credibility to South American contact as theorized by the explorer Thor Heyerdahl.

Easter Island Stone Masonry

Inca Stone Masonry

Adjacent to the wall was a moai statue that had been nearly destroyed thanks to the efforts of 19th century archaeologist William Thompson who wanted a closer look at the wall.

Toppled Moai

Nearby was another moai statue that appeared completed but for some reason was also toppled over. We were to see many moai statues toppled over like some giant vandal had gone through wreaking destruction

Broken Moai

That was enough of Easter Island culture and ruins for the day. We returned to the hotel for a swim and then dined that evening at Mamma Nui restaurant across the street.

Saturday, Jan 9

The archeology survey continues. Today we toured the big dog of all the moai, namely the Rano Raraku quarry where the Easter Islanders dug out and carved most of the statues. Whole fields of them stick up half out of the ground. Reputedly, one can see over four hundred moai in various stages of completion here. We didn't see that many but we saw plenty.

Rano Raraku Quarry

Typical Moai Head

This area provided the classic views of Easter Island that lure thousands of tourists here a year. Of particular interest were the statues that were half-completed and then abandoned for some reason.

Uncompleted Moai

The next question to consider was how the hell were these multi-ton statues, some weighing up to 80 tons, transported to various spots of worship around the island? There are two major theories. One is the tilt walking theory. You know how you can move a large, heavy item by tilting it up on one edge, balancing it and tilting onto another edge and at the same time inching it forward. Some archeologists have demonstrated that by tying ropes to fake statues and then tipping them from one side to another and at the same time advancing it a few inches. Given enough time and patience, you theoretically move these statues for miles. This is the current theory promoted by many archeologists on how they were moved. Maybe.

Walking the Moai

A much more likely theory to me is that they put them on log rollers and rolled them to their destination. This would have required a lot of logs and hence was maybe one reason all the trees on the island were cut down over the centuries. Possibly, the Easter Islanders employed both methods.

Roller Transport

The other major question is why did they carve out these statues at all? Archeologists have noticed similar but much smaller statues on the Marquesan Islands. And they theorize that the Easter Islanders came originally from there.

Marquesan Moai

So why did the Easter Islanders go so big on their moai? One answer is because they could. Gigantism can be a disease. (i.e. mine is bigger than yours.) Also, it was relatively easy carving the soft volcanic bedrock found throughout the island.

Of course, the giant moai probably had some religious or cultural significance but so far nobody can agree on what that was. Perhaps to honor the ancestors.

Mr. Big Head

We spent a couple of hours here hiking around and taking photos. At one point we ran into an older, gray-haired woman with a younger male companion. As we passed by, Yvonne wished them good exploring. The lady simply smiled and nodded. A few minutes later Yvonne declared that this woman was a spitting image of Jane Goodall, the chimpanzee lady from Africa, probably with her son.

I didn't argue. Based on my experience in TV news, when you see a person that looks exactly like a certain celebrity, he or she probably is that celebrity. So Jane Goodall it was.

Next, it was on to the most spectacular sight of all, Ahu Tongariki, where fifteen statues were lined up on an ahu platform facing inland with the ocean as a backdrop. This was a reconstruction job, thanks in part to Japanese funding. You see all these statues had been toppled during the civil wars among the various tribes probably in the 1600s. Further damage to the Ahu occurred in 1960 when a tsunami swept the island.

Ahu Tongariki

Whether this set up reflects the original set up of the statues is just a guess. But the line-up does feature a gigantic statue with a hat like top-knot carved from red volcanic scoria. The top-knot may have functioned as a power symbol. Overall, quite impressive and an ideal tourist poster shot.

Continuing our drive across a small peninsula, we passed numerous other ruins and ahus. We stopped at one spot to examine petroglyphs on a slab, one showing the outline of a double-hulled canoe.

Petroglyphs

We finally wound up at Anakena, the most famous and most swimmable beach on Easter Island. It was very picturesque and very tempting in the blazing sun. But we hadn't brought our swimming suits along. Damn! Maybe another time

So we walked around for a while. According to legend, Anakena was the landing spot for the first settlers of Easter Island. That made sense. It was indeed a nice beach with a placid surf.

Anakena Beach

But the primary reason we were here was to check out the two ahus here with various moai on display including one reputed to be the biggest, the fattest and heaviest on the island.

Big Boy

The other ahu featured a lineup of moai most with impressive top-hats to show how important they were.

Top-Hat Row

After hanging around the beach for an hour or so, we drove back into town to get a better feel for its layout. Aside from a couple of main streets, it was rather disorganized.

The best part was around the waterfront where there were many shops, bars and restaurants. We also saw picturesque excursion boats including dive boats and fishing boats.

Hanga Roa Waterfront

We hung around here for a while having a beer and a sandwich at an outdoor café and then returned to our hotel, had a swim. Later we dined at our shacky roadside restaurant and then retired early.

Sunday, Jan. 10

The next morning, it was a raining hard but we soldiered on, first visiting another area of the island that featured five moai that looked out to sea. Supposedly, these represented the original explorers of Easter Island.

Sea Gazers

Not too impressive compared to what we had seen so far.

Then we checked out the quarry site for the scoria red stone that was carved for top-hats. Plenty of the boulder size scoria was scattered around. A close-up view shows how porous scoria was.

Scoria Boulders

Next, we debated whether or not to explore some of the caves that honeycombed Easter Island. The major one being Ana Te Pahu but it was raining so hard at this point that we kissed it off.

Instead, we drove back to the hotel and chilled until the rain let up. Then in the late afternoon, we drove back through town to the outskirts to take a look at Ahu Tahai, another reconstructed ahu site with a line of statues.

Ahu Tahai

Standing apart from the others was the moai Ahu Ko Ter Riki, which had an impressive top-hat and piercing white eyes made out of seashells and coral that could freak you out.

Ahu Ko Ter Riki

Nobody is quite sure what the white eyes represented other than giving you the illusion that the moai was staring at you as well as signifying a very important person.

This whole restored complex was the work of American archeologist Dr. William Mulloy who completed it in 1974.

In a nearby graveyard, we saw more moai with the piercing eyes. These were all fakes but sitting there in the graveyard they did give you pause.

Fake Moai

Actually, the right time to come here was at sunset but we had come too early for that. However, we did catch a couple of horses peacefully grazing nearby forming a picturesque scene.

Moai & Horses

Later driving around the backroads of town we came across an Easter Island wedding.

Rapa Nui Wedding

I got curious, parked the car and entered the church for a few minutes, pretending I was a guest. I did this much to the chagrin of Yvonne who had told me to stay put in the car but nonetheless accompanied me. However, once inside nobody seemed to mind often smiling broadly at us.

Since it was now early evening, we decided to eat in town and drove back to the waterfront. After walking around a bit, we found an interesting looking restaurant that overlooked the ocean.

Ocean Front Cafe

This time we kept it simple, ordering fish and chips with two large steins of German beer. A German couple seated at the end our long table raised their steins too and offered a salute "Prost."

While their English was not perfect, we fell into conversation about the usual stuff. Where were we from?

How long in Easter Island? What did we think of it? Etc.

They were from a town near Hamburg and both recently retired. They were now on an around the world tour. They had just finished South America. Next up was French Polynesia.

Once again, we fell into conversation about the state of things in Germany and how in their estimation it was going to the dogs. One reason was the unbridled immigration from Poland and the Middle-East.

Yvonne and I had heard this all before and tried to turn the conversation back to touring the world. In the end, they were fascinated by Yvonne's story. About how her family emigrated from Holland in the mid-1950s to the United States.

Towards the end of our conversation, both declared that they really liked us and offered us a place to stay if we were ever near Hamburg, Germany.

The Herr saying, "After all, Hamburg is not too far from Holland. Here is our address. Please keep us in mind. It is refreshing to talk to sophisticated Americans who have traveled abroad." At that point, the Herr handed us a piece of notepaper with their address.

And that was about it. The German couple finished their meal and headed off. Meanwhile, a Polynesian band started playing their enchanting slide guitars and while still sipping on our giant steins of beer, we gazed off out over the ocean watching the evening surfers catching the small waves rolling in. All in all, the Easter Island vibe was in full force.

Monday, Jan 11

The weather was much better. A good day to go exploring but we had already checked out the major sites so we decided to take a look at some minor sights near the hotel. As mentioned before, the hotel was just a few yards from the

seashore. Right outside, we could see a horse taking it easy with a magnificent seascape beyond.

Horse & Sea

Hiking around this shoreline we spotted what looked like a cave to us. We went down a stairway to take a closer look. Actually, it was a sorry looking cave since it was all clogged up with debris. Maybe back in the day it was worthy of hiding Easter Island warriors.

Hiding Cave?

That done, we decided that heck, a one-time look at the Rano Raraku quarry was not enough and drove over there again. It was still impressive with the moai heads sticking up out of the hillside. One group reminded me of a meeting of the board, executive types no less. I also noted the cartoonish features, obviously a distortion of the real features. It lent itself satire.

Chairman of the Board

THE EASTER ISLAND ARMS RACE BEGINS.

You should know that most of these statues extended many feet below the surface of the hill. What we saw was only a fraction of the moai, namely the head and shoulders. Meanwhile, a local guide with no group to guide offered to take photos of Yvonne and me on the hill so I handed over my camera and he snapped away.

On the Scene

We gave him a dollar worth of pesos for his efforts. Perhaps, a word here about the guides that hung around the quarry. We had debated hiring one of them but after listening in on another group of tourists with a guide, we decided that we could do better on our own with our guidebook and prior knowledge of Easter Island. All these guys did was spout the obvious. No doubt there were some real experts around conducting private tours but they were probably out of our price range.

No, we were just happy wandering around on our own and soaking up the atmosphere. We were glad that we had come back here a second time. The Rano Raraku quarry with all its mysterious statues was now permanently etched in our mind.

Well, that took up most of the morning and since the day was bright and warm, we debated what to do next: Drive

to the Anakena beach for a dip or just hit the hotel pool. We opted for the hotel pool with a couple of Mai Tais. Later a nap and then dinner back at Mamma Nui.

That evening we signed up for an "authentic" Polynesian dance show. This involved taking a van from the hotel and winding our way through the outskirts of Hanga Roa to a small amphitheater.

There, a master of ceremony explained some of the aspects of Easter Island Polynesia and their dance culture. He noted that Easter Island while annexed to Chile, had its own laid-back Polynesian culture and that many islanders from French Polynesia were immigrating here to work.

I had indeed noticed that. It was hard to find a purebred Chilean living here. The few that were here were married or somehow related to an Easter Island Polynesian. According to government regulations, a regular Chilean could not live here permanently unless they were a government employee or owned a business or were married to a Polynesian.

And with the end of that little lecture, the place exploded with the ear-shattering beat of the tamure drums. The house lights dimmed and in trooped five lovely wahines swinging their hips.

Dance Troupe

They were a sassy bunch with skimpy bandannas tops and low-slung grass skirts. The guys were great too— Chippendale types. They wore only pareus and were very ferocious with shouts and whoops Right away the tempo was fast. Instant frenzy. The drums had a crackling hollow sound that you could feel in the marrow of your bones.

The girls' feet barely moved and their torsos were nearly rigid. But in between, it was a hotbed of feverish gyrations. The movement was further exaggerated by the flimsy skirts so low on the hips that they appeared to be falling off.

The principal dance movement of the men was a rapid shimmying of the thighs, similar to dogs in heat. The sexual connotation was obvious. However, there was more to it than that. The overwhelming feeling was of a blind, raw life force.

One dancer was a standout. She was a classic Polynesian wahine and she knew how to swing it. The others were O.K. too. Later I got a photo with that dancer and Yvonne now painted up like a native got a photo with the dancing studs.

Dream On

Yvonne & Friends

And that pretty much was the end of our day.

Tuesday, Jan. 12

I tried to take a morning dip in the ocean. But the water was cold, somewhere in the low seventies. I needed a wet suit top. Anyway, my effort was short-lived and I got out immediately. But then I saw kids out there with no wet suit top, bare skin riding boogie boards. They must be used to it, I surmised. And to think, this is the height of summer in these parts when water temperatures are supposedly the highest. The bottom line is don't come to Easter Island for bathlike tropical waters. You need a wet suit for serious endeavors like diving or snorkeling.

A Crappy Beach

Also, be aware that Easter Island has few real beaches aside from Anakena and a much smaller beach called Ovahe. Easter Island has mostly rocky shoreline.

Typical Seashore

However, that doesn't stop the Easter islanders from enjoying the sea. We saw them swimming off any accessible point.

Distant Swimmers

We spent the rest of the day hanging around the hotel with an afternoon excursion into town to look at shops and whatnot. Oh, yes, we did go back over to the Tahai Ceremonial Complex to catch the sunset. It was one of those Rapa Nui iconic moments similar to this scene.

Sunset at Tahai

Later that evening, we had our final dinner at Mamma Nui across the street from the hotel but this time we feasted on lobster and their famous ceviche along with a great bottle of Chilean chardonnay. We also bid the Chilean host and his wife a big goodbye. Yvonne gave him a hug and thanked him for his great meals.

We returned to the hotel, had a Pisco Sour and then retired. Sometime in the middle of the night I woke up and could not go back to sleep. I had a nagging feeling that we were missing something important on Easter Island.

I wasn't quite sure what, but I did get up, pulled on my shorts and T-shirt and went outside into the now cool night. First I scanned the nearby shoreline seeing only the white foam of the surf and hearing a low roar and then I looked up at the night sky. Bong! It was like someone had hit me on the head with a hammer. There before me was a fantastic array of stars that I had never seen before with such stark clarity that it was mind-blowing.

Yvonne had to see this too so I rousted her from bed. After much protest, she threw her bathing robe and flip-flops and joined me outside. The pantheon of stars in the sky took her breath away.

"Allan, I thought we had seen some spectacular night skies before but nothing like this. I get dizzy looking at it. It's almost psychedelic.

Indeed it was. But most importantly we could easily make out the Milky Way with a sharpness never before seen by our eyes except through a telescope in some planetarium show.

Easter Island Milky Way

Later reading up on stargazing in Chile, if the night is not cloudy, Easter Island, because of its remoteness is one of the best stargazing sites in the world, exceeded only by Atacama, in the northern Chilean desert.

In fact, there are many star gazing tours to explain the night skies of Easter Island and to explain how the Polynesians managed to cross vast oceans mainly by star navigation. That was something we probably should have included in our tour of the island. But as it was, just staring at this night sky was inspiration enough.

Wednesday, Jan 13

Not much going on. We hung around the hotel until it was time to leave for our afternoon flight. As mentioned before, a lot of tourists in Chile were on bucket-list tours, some of them were staying at our hotel.

We met one such couple, a British couple. They had done most of South America including Peru, Argentina and Chile. From Easter Island, they were flying on Tahiti and then to New Zealand, Australia, South Africa and Egypt before returning home. It was an eight-month trip.

The sixties-something guy was slumped down on a lobby couch in a dingy white t-shirt and messy hair. He complained to his wife that he was exhausted, had a cold and that all his laundry was dirty. Thankfully, the hotel was taking care of the laundry.

Turning to us, he continued, "Say mate, this travel stuff is not what it is cracked up to be. Thankfully, we've been here a week using Easter Island as a rest stop."

"A rest stop?"

"Of course, mate, we did see all the sights but mostly we just hung around this hotel. We find it very relaxing here."

His wife, who was in better shape and better dressed, concurred with that.

This couple's tired, exhausted condition was common to other around-the-world travelers that we had met. It further convinced me that our three or four-week trips here and there, such as to Europe, Australia, New Zealand, Japan and Chile were the way to go. They were exhausting enough. Return home, rest up, maybe get over some bug contracted somewhere and then a few months later head out again. Someday we wanted to do Africa and especially Egypt but that would have to wait.

***

Around one we drove to the airport. As instructed, I left the keys in the glove compartment of the rental car in the parking lot. The rental car lady had assured me that it would be safe and that she would pick it up later. Car theft was unknown on the island.

As she put it, "What are they going to do with it? Fly it out of the country?"

With our luggage on a cart, we made our way into the terminal. As usual, it was a crowded, chaotic scene but since we were early, it wasn't too bad. By and by, LAN opened their check-in counter and we duly checked in and then killed time by looking at some souvenirs at a nearby kiosk. Most were rather cheesy but we did find a couple of hats emblazoned with the words "Rapa Nui" and below it an outline of a moai. We bought a couple and still have those hats today.

Finally, our flight was called and we boarded another sleek Dreamliner and soon were winging our way across the Pacific with a fully loaded plane. This time I had upgraded to exit seats. During our six-hour flight, we chatted with an older gentleman who was sitting next to us in the window seat. He said he was flying a flock of family and friends back to Santiago after five days in Easter Island implying it was all on his tab.

He was a slick, well-dressed dude in expensive resort clothes and very talkative. He introduced himself as Angelo and claimed he always managed to get an exit seat at the last moment. He said his travel agent in Santiago always got him and his group good seats on supposedly full planes.

I remarked how excellent his English was. He said that was because he had spent twenty years in the U.S. in the 1970s and 1980s. He said he had traded racehorses for a living in the U.S. And indeed I discovered that Angelo did know very well all the horse racing parks in the U.S. including Arlington Park in the Chicago suburbs.

I also noted to myself that Angelo's stay in the U.S. coincided with the Pinochet regime in Chile. I did let him know that I once worked at ABC-TV in Chicago and that we had covered a lot of news of the Pinochet regime during those years. He thought that was interesting but non-committal. Then I mentioned that we visited the Memory Museum in Santiago and viewed their exhibits on the "disappeared" during that time. With this, I got a blank stare and then looking out the window, Angelo said, "Yes indeed, those were troubling times."

Claiming he was simply a businessman during those years, he told us that he had branched out into fields other than horse racing and that now he had a monopoly importing LED lights into Chile. He also added he still had a horse-breeding ranch in southern Chile. Obviously, this guy was a member of the Chilean in-group.

We landed around 9 p.m. and caught a cab to the good old Hilton Garden hotel for a night and day in our plush purgatory. Tomorrow evening we are out of here.

Thursday, Jan 14

We hung around the hotel all day hitting the rooftop pool again, downing a few Pisco Sours and feasting on a late fish lunch with all the trimmings. Then around 7 pm, we took a cab to the airport.

Happily, the international terminal was not too busy but the check-in line was long for our particular flight on American Airlines to Miami.

Finally boarding our 11 PM flight on a rather dated Delta aircraft, certainly not a Dreamliner, we were off for our twelve-hour flight to Miami where we had a two-hour layover before flying off for three hours to Denver, landing sleepless in the bright Colorado sunshine. Isn't travel fun?

And that was it. We retrieved our car from the Canopy Parking lot and drove two hours down to Pueblo where we finally crashed in our home sweet home.

FINAL THOUGHTS

Looking back, I would give this trip to Chile a mixed review with all the hassles, the airline strike and the many surly Chileans that we ran into. The good points included well-maintained major highways, reasonable driving habits, drinkable water, good wine and relatively cheap meals. Occasionally we met nice people, most connected with the tourist trade.

The bad points included general disorganization, family groups that were often loud and obnoxious. Also, we saw and were almost victims to a lot of theft and petty crime in Santiago. We noticed how all the businesses barred their windows and how many homes and hotels had high walls topped with electric wiring and broken glass. We also noticed the Chilean national police force, the Carabineros, were everywhere. In many ways, Chile struck us a still as sort of an underground police state. It seemed at certain points that the Pinochet types still ruled the roost.

Of course, the major positives of this trip was our time in Chilean Patagonia with our excursions to the Torres del Paine, the Magellan Strait and other points of interest near Punta Arenas, a town that we liked and yes, even the fucking penguins deserved their due.

Our days in Easter Island was the stunning capper to this trip. In one way, we did not even associate it with Chile. To us, it was a visitation to an isolated Polynesian wonderland with its mind-boggling array of mysterious moai and laid-back South Seas atmosphere. Easter Island (Rapa Nui) was worth the trip all by itself.

We felt bad that Vanessa didn't get to see it. But as already noted, she is determined to go there. Of course, that would be after she has skied the famous Portillo ski resort in the Andes.

So as a famous stuttering pig once said, "Th-th-th- that's all folks." And so this was the end of our Chilean adventure.

FIN

www.ingramcontent.com/pod-product-compliance
Lightning Source LLC
LaVergne TN
LVHW050525100826
845148LV00002B/438